CW01648338

MARK BRANDON READ

CHOPPER 5

MARK BRANDON READ

CHOPPER 5

DON'T GO BREAKING MY LEGS

JOHN BLAKE

Published by John Blake Publishing Ltd,
3, Bramber Court, 2 Bramber Road,
London W14 9PB, England

www.blake.co.uk

This edition first published in paperback in 2006

ISBN: 978 1 84454 676 3

British Library Cataloguing-in-Publication Data:

A catalogue record for this book is available from the British Library.

Design by www.envydesign.co.uk

Printed in Great Britain by CPI Bookmarque, Croydon, CR0 4TD

3 5 7 9 10 8 6 4 2

Papers used by John Blake Publishing are natural, recyclable products made from wood grown in sustainable forests. The manufacturing processes conform to the environmental regulations of the country of origin.

This book is dedicated to two men from different paths. My father-in-law, E.V. Hodge, a decent and honest fellow, and Big Sam Risovich, 'The American Connection', a friend and a damn good guy.

Adios Amigo.

ABOUT THE AUTHOR

STANDOVER man Mark Brandon Read has done the impossible. He has stayed out of jail for a personal best of two years, fathered a baby named after his old mate, the late gunman Mad Charlie Hegyalji, and has joined Ned Kelly as the only other Australian outlaw whose life has inspired an international motion picture.

His first sojourn into film was the hugely acclaimed Homicide Squad drama documentary *Record of Interview*, based loosely on the untimely death of Siam 'Sammy the Turk' Ozerkam, which played to a captive audience in the Supreme Court – and got five stars from the jury.

CONTENTS

CHAPTER 1

ON THE LAM IN SHEEP COUNTRY

'Mary-Ann was driving a 4.2 litre Jag …
I couldn't help but think she was a
born getaway driver.'

ONE minute I was having a light luncheon inside with Robert Jarvis, the latest member of the Risdon Van Gogh Club, the next I was whizzed out by prison security. No farewells, no cheers, nothing – but I couldn't care less. Freedom is freedom and it is the sweetest thing, any way you get it.

Somehow, I don't think members of the media who had been sweating on my release, then missed it, would agree with that. They were pissed right off. No wonder they missed me outside Risdon. When Peter John Allen was released from Loddon prison, he was picked up in a white limo. When I was released, a white prison bus took me through the gates and dumped me outside the Supreme Court in Hobart. Hardly the way to treat a national icon, I would have thought.

ONLY one member of the media had the right idea. Cops and crims have a code that a favour must be repaid, no matter how long it might take. The first reporters to kidnap me were from Mal Walden's gang at Channel Ten News, and that's because I owed Mal. He did me a good turn in 1978 and called in the favour twenty years later – hence the nickname 'The Don'.

You know how it goes: 'I will do you a favour today and if one day, and I hope that day never comes, I need a favour then I will call on you.' Well, don't ever think the Don won't call on you, because he will.

I could see Mal reading the news in a black shirt and a white tie with a horse's head doing the weather, or a horse's hoof at least. It all goes back to the late 1970s. I wrote to Mal, who was then the newsreader with Channel Seven, and requested some news footage of me that my dad wanted. Most TV types wouldn't have bothered because I was not a hot news story at the time, but Mal did the right thing.

While I was in Risdon he was able to remind me of the past favour. His reporter was the one to get the scoop the day I got out. It didn't stop the others trying. They soon got on the trail, like buzzards circling a buffalo with a bullet in him.

We had a little car chase with my wife, the lovely Mary-Ann, driving a 4.2 litre Jag with plenty of grunt. As we sped along the back roads of Tassie I couldn't help but think she was a born getaway driver.

She was behind the wheel of her beloved old Jag, like the ones the Great Train Robbers used. Here was my law-abiding wife, driving like she was part of the Kray gang, trying to burn off a TV crew. I didn't know whether to laugh, cry or shoot. So much for my idea of quietly slipping out into the real world without too much fuss and bother.

The second lot to get me after a fifty-kilometre car chase were Kellie Russell of Channel Seven News and her crew. It was madness. Didn't these people remember that the last time I got excited in a motor vehicle my former friend and serial liar, Syd Collins, copped a bullet in the belly and I copped a bum rap and an indefinite jail sentence? A lot of crims copped a bum rap in jail, or so I'm told, but that was just in the showers.

We were at a disadvantage. We were in a Jag that I had spent $17,000 rebuilding, while they drove a hire car, which they considered they were duty bound to drive to death. Every rock that spat up and hit our car was $25 into the panel beater's pocket. When they hit something it was the height of good humour.

We pulled over and young Kellie offered to pay for lunch and drinks, courtesy of Channel Seven. She got her interview and I got a couple of drinks and a rump steak. Seemed a fair deal to me.

At least Kellie had the good manners to buy me a beer.

'Do you have anything to add in closing, Chopper?' was her last question on the interview.

I looked the long, skinny, blonde kid up and down and replied, 'Yeah, get yourself a bloody exercise programme.'

She nearly fell over and that part of the interview was cut out but she went straight back to Melbourne and enrolled in a gym and, I'm told, has shaped up quite nicely. So much so that I reckon I'll be a tad more polite when we next meet. Ha ha.

12 FEBRUARY 1998. I had been at the Hobart Casino at Wrest Point most of the night with one bottle of vodka settled into me and a second bottle trying to stay down but threatening to come back up with my first feed outside jail in six years. I'd won and then lost I don't know how much money.

Early that morning I'd woken up in the small township of Richmond, Tasmania, badly hung over, to be greeted with a media frenzy. Every mob that had missed me at Risdon, and hadn't got there in time for the car chase across country, was trying to make up for lost time.

A Miss Jackson was desperate to see me, along with a Miss this and a Miss that from this or that news and/or current-affairs programme.

Oh, how they love a man with no ears. Right up until the interview is over, at least, all these pretty perfumed things chasing me in their high heels and outfits chosen by TV wardrobe assistants. They are kids, more frightened of coming back to their office without a story and getting knocked off by another reporter than getting the real truth.

They smile and flirt, act wounded and make promises they can't keep. Dim as they are, they know that a known crim who can make a smart-arse crack in front of a camera is much better value than a politician with no dash, so the old Chopper was the biggest 'news' story of the day. And I was like an 18-year-old virgin: the more I said 'no', the more they chased me.

I knew that if I rang them up in a few months for a favour they wouldn't return the calls, but at the time I was as hot as Bill Clinton. And, after all those years in jail, nearly as horny.

CHAPTER 2

THE HARD FACTS

'I would get a call from old friends and, sadly, I would then know that some old associate was a walking corpse.'

IT is half past one in the morning with Mary-Ann asleep and my two cats Poop Foot and Ernie sitting with me by the fire, keeping me company while I write. Between us I suspect we have about twenty seven lives but I fear I may have used nearly all my quota. I am three quarters of the way through a bottle of Grants Scotch Whisky – William Grants Family Reserve, to be exact.

I've been out of jail for a year and my weight has gone from twelve and a half stone to seventeen and half stone. I was a vegetarian when I was inside and worked out every day, and now I'm a middle-aged fat slob chicken farmer badly in need of – you guessed it – an exercise programme.

Sorry, Kellie, I should have kept my fat gob shut.

This book was to be a crime fiction or faction book. It was to be called *The Calabrian Contract,* and be about the life and death of Melbourne gangster Alphonse Gangitano.

The death of Alphonse, in my opinion, was the height of good humour – but then my old mate Charlie Hegyalji got hit as well. Poor Mad Charlie gets it, then bing, bang, bing, all over Melbourne old friends and enemies were getting it in the neck, and the back, and sometimes in the belly.

I then said to myself, 'Myself,' I said, 'there is no need to do a fiction book on Alphonse and his mob because the truth about the Australian underworld is weirder, funnier and bloodier than anything Hollywood could dream up.' I also know there is only one person who can write about the storm from inside the eye of the cyclone. And that is exactly what I'm bloody well going to do. So if you want to know what happens with crims in every part of the country, just put your seat in the upright position and get ready for take-off.

Every time something new happened young Kellie Russell would ring me up and ask my opinion on what was going on. It got to the stage that when Mary-Ann said Kellie was on the phone I would go and put on a fresh black T-shirt and go into mourning straight away.

'Come on, Chop Chop, what's going on?' she would ask in her best Woodward and Bernstein style. And, of course, under such pressure I was sure to tell her exactly what I knew.

Even in rural Tasmania I would sometimes get a call from old friends and, sadly, I would then know that some old associate was a walking corpse. There was no point telling old Charlie to watch his back. When your dance card is full there's nothing much you can do about it other than retire and take up chicken farming. From assault and battery to battery chickens. That's a joke – actually they're free range. Naturally. Having spent so long in a cage myself I think it's a crime if the animals don't have a little freedom.

The truth is if you told a donkey what I knew he'd kick you in the head for pulling his leg. Crime and criminals and the world they live in do not walk hand in hand with the truth, and when big things happen in that world to those people, the police and the media and the rest of the outside looking in all expect there to be a big reason. A big reason for a big police investigation, a big reason for a big story. No one wants to hear that Mr Big was really Mr Not So Bloody Big at all and that he got knocked for an even smaller reason.

Let's face it, Ned Kelly was only a trumped-up horse thief who rode about Victoria with a bucket on his head. The truth is always smaller than the story, but people love legends so the criminal world, like a lot of other scallywags in the history books, has provided us all with legends, myths, real life, true blue fictional characters.

How do I know? Well, I'm Chopper Read. Would I tell a lie?

Alphonse Gangitano used this to shroud himself in the myth of the Mafia. That same Mafia that used the magic of human fear to turn a lie into a legend, which can be done by small men if the men wishing to do it are hell bent on achieving a result at any price.

A group of dagoes with a few guns is hardly a big deal, but a group of dagoes with guns and with the funny handshake of the Mafia is supposed to be a big deal and we should all get down on our knees before them. I'm not saying that a legend is nothing but a pack of lies. What I am saying is that one cannot create a legend without the help of a pack of lies. We start with some truth, then add lies to build it up. Everyone adds another story to the story until we end up with a skyscraper of a legend. The lies are the glue that hold the whole thing together and as a result the lies within each and every legend are the most secret and protected part of the structure.

Take the Mafia – please. All jokes aside, it began as a group of honourable men who fought for the poor and then it got corrupted into a crime gang. Then idiots like Alphonse tried to jump on board wearing imported clothes, eating garlic and kissing people on the cheeks, and sometimes on the face too.

Eventually the fiction becomes a reality, but Alphonse didn't flick to the end of the book of his own life of make-believe. It ended with him being shot. Everyone knew what was on the last page but the poor fat slob himself. His fantasy became reality and he ended up dead.

I guess this book, if you bother to read further, is meant to help the reader unravel the sticky mess that holds the legend together. If Alphonse had known what was going to happen would he have lived his life differently, I wonder? I suspect not. He got his picture in the paper. Some people who believed the crap actually treated him with respect. If it wasn't for the myth he would have been just another used-car salesman in a bad suit.

I WAS just re-reading the transcript of my evidence in the inquest of the suspected death of Christopher Dale Flannery. Quite comic reading, if I do say so myself. I was toying with the thought of using it in the book when my train of thought was interrupted (actually it was totally derailed) when a former Miss Nude Australia, Alison 'Candy' Downes, came over to walk her dog on the farm. Her dog, Scruffy, and my little puppy, Billy, get on well, so what do I do: continue writing or walk across the paddocks with her? You're quite right, walking is good exercise, and I need it. Walking the dog beats spanking the monkey any day.

Most men my age would be happy to walk Miss Nude Australia across the paddocks with a dog or two, giving new meaning to the words 'watch those puppies bounce'. We had two puppies, a fine pussy and half a mongrel all out in the fresh air.

I was in a fine mood until I got home to find the Yankee Clipper, Jolting Joe Di Maggio, had passed away. The keeper of the Marilyn Monroe flame has gone to join the candle in the wind. So why does a scarred-up old chicken farmer like me shed a tear? Well, maybe I'm just an old sentimental softie underneath. I guess that is why I treat the deaths of so-called Melbourne Mister Bigs so lightly. Their impact, if any, was only in the town they lived in.

To hit the big time you have to hit the world, and no Australian crim has ever done that yet. The Kangaroo Gang, with due respect to my old mate Ray Chuck, was world class – but they were just glorified shoplifters over there, and knocking off stuff from some French department store hardly puts them in the Capone class.

Yes, I'm sorry, that goes for Ned Kelly too. No Australian outside of acting, sports, singing and movie production has yet to hit the world – and certainly no crim. Well, not as yet. So you might forgive my view when I write about these wombats. I have a global perspective, while most of them are nothing but navel lint.

LET us start with Chris Flannery. Mr so-called Rent a Kill – more like Rent a Dill if you ask me. And you have asked me, or you wouldn't have got this far into the book.

Think about it for a moment, you've paid your money for this book, or had it given to you by someone who doesn't like you much, or you've knocked it off. Whatever, if you don't like it already you can throw it in the bin, but then you'll never know how it ends and you won't know if I've mentioned you in the next 200-odd (very odd) pages.

I pause now to yawn about Flannery and, having yawned ... I lost my train of thought and decided to go to the pub. I'd rather drink than write about non-events, yesterday's has-beens ...

I'VE returned from the Richmond Arms Hotel (burp) totally shattered and in no mood to write anything. I'm legless, but then again, so is Chris, and less a few other things too. Ha ha.

I was sitting at the bar having ordered my third Melbourne Bitter and having lost my sixth game of Keno. I was wearing Blue Yakka work pants and a white T-shirt and an old pair of slip-on shoes Mad Charlie gave me in 1987. The shoes were holding up well, better than Mad Charlie, as it turned out. The Richmond Arms does not demand formal attire from its patrons, hence I went for the smart casual look.

Although I can find my own company quite fascinating, I could hardly not notice when a young, well put together girl walked past me wearing a skin-tight black outfit. She got about five or six feet past me and did an about-face, then walked back past me again to rejoin her friends. She had an arse and a set of hips on her that swung about in a manner likely to cause injury. Da boom, da boom, you know the drill. You don't have to be Chris Flannery to be stiff, if you know what I mean. I'm sure she got back to her friends and said in a loud whisper, 'What? The fat bloke in the white T-shirt?'

'Yeah,' said someone, 'that's him.'

I ignored this slur, sucked in my gut and looked about to see if anyone else in the bar was wearing a white T-shirt. I was the only one.

'That's him,' said another voice.

'Bullshit,' said another.

'Check him out.'

I sensed movement as the swinging hips swung past me yet again, this time standing next to me at the bar and asking for a bottle of sauce to go with whatever food she was eating with the rest of the wombats she was sitting with.

I could sense her looking at me. I stared straight ahead still with my gut sucked in and polished off my can. Then she turned and walked away. I got up and walked out. The fat bloke in the white T-shirt quietly shuffled off down the road and wandered back to his chicken farm to continue writing this book, only to receive yet another phone call from the movie people wanting me to sign yet another contract.

I've taken a few contracts in my time but nothing like the one the movie people keep running past me. I now realise a Sydney trendy in a turtleneck sweater backed by a group of lawyers with more time on their hands then sense is far more ruthless than the Lygon Street mob.

So far I've signed over everything bar my eyes and I'd be willing to give those too if it made them happy. I can't give them my ears because they've already been taken.

Movie people don't mean to be rude, but they do tend to take themselves a tad seriously. The other fellow's point of view is a mystery to them unless it agrees with their own. They say to me 'Yes, Chopper' or 'Yes, Mark, we can hear you talking' or 'we can hear what you're saying'.

What they really mean is, we can hear you knocking, but you can't come in. The funny thing about rope is that if you give people enough of it they insist on hanging themselves, and my smiling face and readiness to agree to the most insane arrangement is not politeness; it's rope.

So the fat bloke in the white T-shirt agrees to sign away the rights to his own story so that others can get rich. People are concerned that I might make money out of a film about me, based on books I wrote myself. Silly me.

Anyway, back to that dog Flannery. Chris Flannery was never a tough crim or a hard man. He was only ever a mouth. He couldn't fight. His reputation for violence first reached my ears, when I still had them, back when I was in my teens. Flannery gave it to a very well-known Melbourne street fighter at a party in St Kilda with a broken beer bottle. I won't name the other bloke, as naming people in matters Flannery could involve them in legal trouble. A lot of people have come to learn that, so I'll just call him Ray.

Well, Ray had begun drinking at the Waterside Hotel in Melbourne at 6am. The Waterside was an early opener. Now this is not something I have picked up second hand, as Cowboy Johnny Harris and my good self had been drinking right there with Ray. He was rolling pissed drunk, as Johnny and I both were by midday. Ray piled into a taxi and went off to Fitzroy – The Champion Hotel via the Builders Arms, I'm told. Which were by no means trendy inner-suburban wine bars in those days, I can assure you. Anybody who could hold his own in the bar at either joint was no sugar plum fairy.

Johnny and I went back home, slept and awoke around 8pm,

refreshed and ready to head to some mad party in St Kilda. I must say, I didn't spend that much time out of jail in the seventies and eighties, but when I was out we had a bit of fun.

Owen Boston and Jack Nicola invited us to the turn. Lennie Loft and his crew would be there and most of the Prahran crew, as well as Mad Charlie and his lot. We went to the Chevron nightclub first to fuel up. Big Ray was fast asleep on the footpath outside the Chevron. It was Mad Charlie who bundled Ray into a car and told Archie to drive. Big Ray was out of it. He had already been in a punch-up with Steve O'Brien and Ronnie Walker in Chapel Street, Prahran, and had ten shades of shit smacked out of him.

Poor Ray was having a bad day. It was time for bed. So you can imagine my surprise when at about 2am me and the Cowboy got to the party in St Kilda and learnt that Big Ray had been attacked with a broken bottle ... while he slept in one of the spare bedrooms. He had been taken to the Alfred Hospital.

Who did it? Big tough Chris Flannery and the Sydney Road crew, that's who. Sydney Road, Brunswick, is a long way to come from just to sneak a go at a bloke while he sleeps. It turned out Ray had led the gang that gangbanged some bloke's sister from that side of town. I didn't say Ray was a nice person who didn't deserve a flogging, I'm just saying Flannery attacked him when he was more dead than alive. Also the 'pack rape' took place in a massage parlour in Coburg, so it hardly falls into the category of deflowering the singing nun.

When it comes to matters of forcible sex Chris couldn't really take the high moral ground. Flannery was himself a hetero and a homo rapist. He had done it to both good-looking girls and boys, and he built a reputation on violence toward both sexes. Being a firm believer in equal opportunity he'd attacked as many females as males. I didn't know Flannery and he didn't know me. We had seen each other, but he never came too close. I mustn't have been his type.

We moved in the same circles and I think we knew that if those circles clashed it would end in tears. His, for instance.

You see, I didn't have to stay out of his way. He made it his business to stay out of mine. But we knew a lot about each other. One young man on the way up, likes to know the business and the doings of other young men on the way up, and when I was sixteen I had men in their twenties asking curious questions about me.

You see, the Chopper was coming up too fast and too hard. When I was sixteen Flannery's reputation in Melbourne overshadowed my own for violence. When I was seventeen it didn't. You can achieve a lot in the underworld in a year if you are keen and a little crazy.

By the time I was eighteen Flannery, as far as street violence went, was a has-been. The Chopper reigned and that was that.

Flannery was in and out of prison and trying to enter the world of the Hollywood nightclub gangster, but blood still ruled on the Melbourne streets in those days. Shitkickers who ran nightclubs and massage parlours and got their photos taken wearing suits were considered as dangerous as a poodle with false teeth.

In 1977, when I got out of H Division at Pentridge, Flannery was the part-owner of a St Kilda nightclub. It was a natural career move for him. He was more at home under a silver disco ball than with real hard men. Nightclub owners and pimps, or hoons as we called them then, were all the same. A crim who ran a nightclub that hired off-duty policemen to work as bouncers – well, you had to be half a fucking policeman to begin with, didn't you? That was our attitude, anyway.

Flannery ran the place, but when any of the heavy crews walked in it was free drinks, all on Flannery, but he was elsewhere. The Melbourne crims wiped their bottoms on Flannery and blokes like him, so Sydney was the place to go. It's always been the place where failed Melbourne crims can make good, and the fact that they continue to do so speaks volumes for Sydney, home of the Gay Mardi Gras.

Flannery tried to kill the undercover copper, Mick Drury, but he botched the job. He decided to be king of the kids but he was running red hot and disappeared in May, 1985 and, as everyone knows, his body was never found. Many people think they know what happened to him. Maybe he is in a three-piece band with Elvis and Lord Lucan. But I understand and still maintain that his body finished up in a tree shredder.

Many people poo-poo my ideas on this and other matters, but the Sydney coroner who had to investigate what happened had the brains to send his people to visit me in Risdon prison in September, 1994.

The lawyers were paid more than a grand a day. I got a cheese sandwich. I told them that a man who could be trusted told me a well-known Melbourne criminal hit Flannery with a meat cleaver in a car near Seymour and then put him through a tree shredder.

CHAPTER 3

ALPHONSE: FROM HEADLINES TO HEADSTONES

'I had no respect for the wobbly-bottomed dago from the word go.'

LET us now move toward the rather unsavoury topic of Alphonse Gangitano. Well, what can I say about Alphonse? First off, he's dead and I'm not. And that's a good start.

I knew him since he was sixteen, when he knocked about Johnny's Green Room in Carlton. Mad Charlie introduced us. I sold the prick his first sawn-off shotgun. I didn't want it, Charlie didn't want it, so we offloaded it on the posh Italian kid from the flash suburbs. We called Al 'Posh' because he went to a posh private school and was a real spoilt brat with a tough-guy complex. Everyone knows the type: a bully to kids he could beat and a suckhole to kids he couldn't.

It was funny. I had no respect for the wobbly bottomed dago from the word go. I didn't think much of Alphonse, yet my mate Charlie saw something in Alphonse that I didn't.

Mad Charlie had a sort of strange respect for Alphonse, but Charlie was always the thinker, the would-be politician, the budding businessman, even then. Alphonse made me laugh. He gave himself the air of a young Mafia boy on the way up and dropped the names of older men, Italian men, Calabrian and Sicilian men. He was a boy in a man's world and it would end up costing him his life.

The thing was, I grew up in Thomastown in the northern suburbs, the dago capital of Melbourne back then. I went to school with the sons and grandsons of these old Italian guys Alphonse was talking about. Alphonse dropped these old guys' names five to six years before he ever got to meet them. I know because I asked them.

Alphonse was always a salesman at heart. Sharp, well dressed, well spoken, fairly well educated, from a fairly well-to-do family, but a fucking salesman. That's all. He sold shit and told people it was chocolate. Big deal. Mad Charlie really was a good crim, but Alphonse had conned him, so I've got to take my hat off to him. He was very good at what he did, while it lasted.

Holy shit. I have to put my pen down. One of my devil traps just went off. It's 2am and I've got three Tassie Devil traps set near my chicken house, just to keep them away from my lovely layers. I'll just go and check. Just re-read the last few pages, grab a beer and I'll be back with you. Have a cup of tea or a piss and then we'll move on.

SORRY about the break in transmission. I'm back again. Poop Foot, my cat, went in to grab the meat and got himself caught in the cage. He is now by the fire with his brother Ernie.

Stupid cats, they are locked in the house for the night now, so we can get on with it and leave the Devils in peace outside. The Tasmanian variety, that is.

Back to Alphonse. As I said, we weren't always enemies. I didn't respect him, but we were friendly enough and together with Mad Charlie and others we hit our fair share of massage parlours and nightclubs, and got into hotel brawls and so on. The sort of shit all self-respecting young blokes did in the seventies before they invented Nintendo and Gameboys and needle exchanges. I was nineteen, Charlie was seventeen and Alphonse was around the same age.

He could have been younger, I don't know. I do know that 1974 was the last year Alphonse and I called each other mates.

I remember I used to call him 'Fat Boy'. He had a fair bit of baby fat on him back then. Probably from his mama's Italian cooking. She was always fond of her little boy, and he was fond of her.

Charlie had the torch when me, him and Alphonse were robbing the home of a parlour owner thanks to a tip-off from Al. Mad Charlie had turned off the alarm and the power. It was pitch black. We were in the bedroom when Charlie said, 'What the light shines on is mine.' We cracked up. Charlie was holding the torch and what the light shone on was his.

Alphonse didn't want to be there. He had given Charlie the mail on the burg, but didn't expect to be invited along. I didn't want to be there, either, so when Alphonse said 'someone is coming', it was just the excuse we needed. Charlie had to escape into the night with us, empty handed.

Then, with Alphonse and myself drinking with about twenty others at a St Kilda nightclub, Charlie went back alone and emptied the place out of approximately thirty grand cash and over a hundred grand in valuables. Alphonse and myself couldn't say a word. Neither of us were break-and-enter men.

Charlie had hit the place alone and done well. Alphonse and I had got out too soon the first time round. Alphonse was the gangster, I was the mad man but Charlie was the money maker, even then. Alphonse and I got all the headlines, but Charlie got all the money.

So there you have it. Even as kids we were shaping up into what we would all later become. Me, I'm just a survivor these days. Now Al and Charlie are both dead and the only thing I ambush are Tassie Devils in the chicken house.

DURING the 1974 parlour war in Melbourne, Alphonse used Mad Charlie to great effect. I didn't know it at the time, but Charlie was acting even then in Big Al's interest against parlour owners south of the river.

I remember parlours around Carlton, Fitzroy and West Melbourne were out of bounds, according to Charlie.

I robbed them anyway, without Charlie, only to have Mad Charlie fly into some insane rage claiming that my actions would fuck up his friendship with the Italians.

Dave the Jew thought this was high comedy and we would tell Charlie to piss on the Italians. Charlie would laugh and agree with us. It was in the days before political correctness.

'Yeah, Chopper, fuck 'em, what have they ever done for me?' he'd say. But that night Charlie would be over in Carlton having coffee and cake with Fat Boy Alphonse, saying sorry.

In those days Alphonse should have laid off the cake, but what does it matter? Cholesterol didn't kill him, unless the mate who later shot him blew him away with eight cheeseburgers in the back.

Big Al didn't own the clubs I robbed, but he was copping a regular sling from the owners. The parlour managers weren't Italian but the buildings were owned by Italians. It was a bit hard for a nineteen-year-old kid, as I then was, to work out. I was robbing from parlours, not working at the UN.

Later it would be drug dealers, but the aim of the game was the same. Black money and plenty of it, from places and faces that made it unlikely people would be too quick to scream to the cops.

Then came the Cindy affair.

Alphonse was seeing this twenty-seven-year old prostitute named Cindy. She worked in a parlour in Carlton and, yes, she had all the right stuff. Bleach-blonde hair, long legs, big tits and a Barbie-doll face.

This chick was ten or so years older than Alphonse. She was working for Jeff Lamb, the biggest parlour owner during the 1970s, and was meant to be on with him. She was also a favourite dirty girl for a handful of well-known crims from Footscray, and the step-daughter of a painter and docker. A top pedigree.

Cindy was also being screwed by various police. She was, dare I say it, a busy little beaver. Many girls have been fixed up by both sides of the law over the years, including Kath Pettingill before she got old and one-eyed. All in all, Cindy knew more people than Alphonse and had a much stronger power base but, as the saying goes, or should go, 'just cos you suck off a few gangsters don't mean you are one'.

Cindy and Alphonse had words about Cindy seeing a policeman and Big Al punched her through a glass shower screen, then grabbed her by her hair and ran her face across the broken glass.

Cindy's working days were over. Within three hours Alphonse was being threatened by a crew of crims from Footscray right out of his league, so who does he run to? Not his Italian mates, and not his own crew in Carlton. He runs to Mad Charlie. Why? Because Charlie had the Jew and me on side.

Charlie's crew, being us, had total disregard for the criminal old school, so with Charlie promising to sort it out, Alphonse went home and remained there.

It was me and the Jew who went to Footscray on what we thought was a personal favour for Charlie. No mention of Alphonse. We were doing a good turn for Mad Charlie who was also home in bed. We smashed these pricks in Footscray so hard with claw hammers that to this day I still don't know how any of them lived.

Two days later Alphonse and Mad Charlie were out from under their blankets and we went drinking in hotels in Footscray again. It was only then that I knew it was all a favour for Alphonse. Thank God the Jew wasn't with us when I was told or the story of Mad Charlie and Alphonse would have ended then and there. The Jew, bless his heart, can be particularly excitable, especially when he doesn't take the medication.

As it was, my lukewarm friendship for this Italian pretender was beginning to turn into a very strong dislike. I suppose I could list pub and club brawls where Mad Charlie and myself had backed the dago turd up, but why bother? The last time I saw Alphonse in 1974 he had just lifted $200 out of some poor girl's handbag at a Melbourne nightclub, and him and Mad Charlie and a crew of Carlton leftovers were off to spend the profits. I declined and went to join my own crew with Dave the Jew at a club in Prahran. Alphonse would run true to form for the next 24 years, always hitting the easy targets.

I wasn't to see him face to face again until 1977.

IF Melbourne ever had a true Mr Big of crime, of vice at any rate, Peter Thomas Evan Rand deserves the championship belt. Not that you'd think so to meet him. A homosexual millionaire from an old-money Melbourne family, the son of the late Sir Thomas Rand, Peter the Poof, or 'Pam' Rand as he was comically known, controlled Melbourne's vice world with a perfumed lace hanky held in an iron fist.

He passed away on 7 October 1997, aged 74, after a long battle with cancer. I've attempted to include Peter in other books but doing so without hurting the old bloke or his rather powerful old money, landed gentry, Melbourne Club family was a delicate matter.

You see, Peter knew where all the bodies were buried and never told on anyone, so to nominate him publicly as the Vice Queen of Melbourne while he was still alive would be bad manners. He died supposedly leaving behind only a $20 million fortune. Personally, I always thought Peter had more. He must have fallen on hard times.

Peter owned buildings and property and rented them out the same for the use of prostitution. He also owned brothels and gay night clubs in Hawaii. I will say more about Peter as I go along but in telling of his vice and crime interests I don't want anyone to think that I'm being disloyal to a dear old friend. Because of his sense of comedy and eccentricity, Peter would forgive me, I'm sure. I'm told people mellow in temper and mood after their death, so I'm sure Peter would smile on this.

I first met Peter Rand when I was working as a bouncer with Cowboy Johnny Harris at Mae West's nightclub in Oban Street, South Yarra.

Peter was having the shit kicked out of him in the street and Johnny and I came to his rescue. This was 1970. When Mad Charlie and myself began robbing massage parlours in 1973 and 1974 Peter called us to his South Yarra mansion in Domain Road. His bodyguard at that time was an old hood named Ronnie.

Now, Ronnie worked within the prostitution industry, allegedly, for John Eric Twist. Jackie Twist, an old-time dockie and underworld killer. So if Ronnie Banks worked for Twist – then who did Twist work for? Only Peter Rand really knew.

Ronnie was meant to give Mad Charlie and myself a fright while Peter gave us a good talking to. We had just recently made a frightful mess of the Crest massage parlour. Peter agreed that if I pleaded guilty to the Crest he would make the other eighty-odd outstanding armed robberies vanish. I did and he did. He must have been a magician.

'Sorry, my dear, but there is no other way,' he said.

'Kill Peter Rand,' said Dave the Jew, 'that's another way.'

'No,' said Charlie, and I was conned into pleading guilty.

Mad Charlie and Garry the Greek, along with Mad Archie, pleaded not guilty and walked with Peter's help. I'd been tricked. Dave the Jew was nearly as unimpressed as me and visited Peter Rand – and then I received a visit from a lawyer along with $25,000 in compensation money and an urgent note to visit Peter as soon as I got out, along with a note requesting me to tell the Jew that all was well.

Dave was a severe negotiator who sometimes seemed disappointed when negotiations didn't break down and violence had to be employed. We all know what stress these children of holocaust survivors are under. Some of them are not fussy about who they take revenge on, in the absence of Nazis. Especially Dave.

He always liked the idea of employing plan B immediately and, rather than cutting to the chase, he would rather chase someone to cut. I was pretty easygoing back then and, given the twenty five grand sling, agreed to bide my time.

It seemed that around that time Peter had also gained a new friend he didn't need, Alphonse Gangitano. Peter allowed Gangitano to manage and control Rand-owned clubs, parlours and property in Richmond, West Melbourne and Carlton. Have all these years clouded my memory or did Peter have a little crush on pretty, porky Al?

Peter Rand's vice empire was being eaten away by the rats. Peter fled to the USA – well, Waikiki in Hawaii at any rate, and sold off most of the buildings his parlours and clubs were in. Peter doubled his money on the property sales, but lost his grip on the criminal vice network he had built.

However, he has his place in Melbourne's secret history as the man behind the introduction of homosexual brothels and bath houses into that city. It was, back then, an area no criminal would touch for fear of being tainted with the poof tag. Peter ended up making more out of gay clubs and brothels than he did out of land and property deals. He returned to Melbourne in 1976 and made it known that his interest in the vice world was no more. He was going straight, in a manner of speaking. However, Alphonse and his crew continued to stand over Peter.

Somehow, Alphonse had gained the nod of approval from old Jackie Twist, who had also turned on Peter the Poof. Mad Charlie was in jail over a rape charge, and Dave the Jew wouldn't work for a poof. The Jew would have described himself as homophobic if he knew what it meant. In those days it was enough to say he didn't like poofs.

At the time I wasn't due out for about a year. So Peter Rand found himself the victim of standover tactics and handing over large amounts of cash to Alphonse for a full year until I got out. Of course, I wasn't all that pleased with Peter myself. He had handed several hundred thousand dollars to Melbourne criminals, along with control of clubs and parlours. I'd copped $25,000 compensation for doing prison time I didn't need to do. I'd been doing porridge while he'd been eating it. I'd spent $20,000 on firearms and given the other five grand away to friends in need.

I walked out of prison in 1977 gun rich and cash poor. Peter Rand wanted me to fight his battles for him on the strength of the $25,000 I'd already been paid. Peter wanted revenge, but would not hand anyone a penny more, or so he said. All I had to do was sort out the Gangitano matter and Peter would see me right. I contacted Mad Charlie, who was still in jail. Even inside he was a man of some influence.

'Fuck Pam Rand,' said Charlie, a man of few words and most of them obscene. 'That old poof don't own or control nothing no more.'

Dave the Jew agreed.

But I wasn't sure. I don't know why but I felt sorry for old Peter Rand and agreed to go along and talk to Alphonse at the Dover Hotel in Carlton. Peter Rand was living in his fortress-like white mansion at 268 Domain Road, South Yarra, totally alone and in fear. I don't know why I felt sorry for him, but there you go. Maybe it was my Christian upbringing.

'Why am I helping you,' I said to Peter, 'you old poof?'

'Because I remind you of your mother, darling,' said Peter.

For some reason I sensed that if I took old Peter's side against his tormentors I'd earn myself a powerful and blood-loyal friend. So, in the face of all sound advice and without the Jew's help I went to see Fat Boy Alphonse. Chopper Read fighting the good fight on behalf of an old queen, old enough to be my father – or, in his words, my mother.

How would I ever live this one down? I cut my teeth on bashing faggots. The whole situation was insane, but I knew if I didn't move against Alphonse we would all end up working for the fat-arsed dago, so off I went.

I MET with Alphonse and his crew upstairs at the Dover Hotel. Big Al and his team seemed pleased to see me. It's sad to look back and see it's gone … not Big Al, the pub.

Conversation that night ranged from Mad Charlie, who Alphonse believed would join his crew when he got out of Pentridge, to Peter Rand, who was secretly financing a major heroin venture, as well as placing Alphonse in control of large massage-parlour interests. Big Al said Shane Goodfellow was also joining his crew.

I doubted aloud that Mad Charlie would ever team up with

Alphonse. Big Al accepted this. I then said Shane Goodfellow was a wombat and as soon as I saw him I'd flog him.

Goodfellow could beat Big Al in a fight and my dismissing Goodfellow as a total loser insulted Gangitano. It was a calculated insult. Then I told Al to drop off Pam Rand and explained that any money anyone could squeeze out of Peter Rand was only ever petty cash to Peter. He would probably outlive us all and would make a better friend than an enemy. I told Alphonse that if he fucked with Peter he fucked with me and if he fucked with me he had better attach a toilet roll to the side of his head coz I'd use his mouth to piss in. It seemed to me a sound negotiating tactic.

I finished my seventh pint of beer. I drank seven pots an hour back then. I excused myself to go to the shithouse. I walked into the toilet and locked the door, pulled my pants down, put my revolver on the floor and proceeded to squeeze out a prison officer when, all of a sudden, there was a smash and a crash and the toilet door got kicked in.

All I remember was fists and feet. All I wanted to do was get off that toilet and get my pants up. Pain was nothing compared with public embarrassment. I got my pants up with my face running red with a river of blood.

I pissed my pants. I then replaced shock with self-defence and started tossing return punches. I never was really quick but even my enemies would admit then that when I hit, you stayed hit. I felt my left fist connect with a mouth and my right fist hit a nose.

I heard two sets of squeals like someone had just stuck a knife up a puppy's arse and with my eyes full of blood I charged out screaming and tossing punches.

Evidently two bouncers came to help me and I floored both of them. Nothing personal. You just keep throwing punches until you can't. Big Al and his crew had attacked and ran away, leaving me to toss punches blindly, convinced I was fighting the whole pub.

PETER RAND'S problems no longer mattered. Alphonse had laid hands on my person. He now had two choices. He could hide or he could die. Big Al hid well. Later, he would prove to be just as adept at the other.

The Dover Hotel was shot up the night after as well as the homes of several of Big Al's crew. I nearly got Gangitano in a laneway in Carlton. He had a handgun. As it happened, it was the same .38 revolver I'd put on the floor of the toilet at the Dover Hotel. I was driving Pam Rand's 1975 model Grand AM Pontiac motor car. I didn't have a licence to drive, but then again I didn't have a licence to carry a gun, or a licence to shoot fat dagos either. That was living in the Seventies, doing the Lygon Street Limbo.

Big Al and two of his retards moved up behind the car as I was getting out. They thought they had me in the bag except for one little detail – I was carrying my dad's – pump action shotgun, fully loaded with SG shells.

For those who don't know, SGs have a few slugs the size of ball bearings on the heavy side of buckshot, and are used sometimes for shooting pigs. Which made them perfect for Porky Al.

I pumped off two shots as the dago and his mates ran off down the laneway and into the night. Big Al dropped the .38 revolver he was carrying, and I picked it up. That's how I know it was the one I'd lost on the night at the Dover.

As it happened, 'Pam' Rand's problem with Alphonse became a side issue, as in any criminal blood war sides are taken and the reasons for the original dispute are lost. People take sides out of loyalty or because they see some advantage for themselves, never because of right and wrong.

Big Al could no longer risk even talking to Peter Rand let alone attempting to do business with him for fear that anyone associated with me could unknowingly lead Alphonse to his death. Mad Charlie being the rare exception as Charlie, always the politician, remained both my friend and Alphonse's.

Charlie was a one-off. Everyone liked him and even the coppers thought he was funny, but he used his charm to stay ahead of the pack, or so he thought.

However, in 1987 Charlie was, I believe, attempting to set me up for Alphonse. Oh, what a web we weave. That's life. Or should I say, death?

PAM RAND felt the whole Chopper Read – Alphonse thing was all done by me to protect him and in gifts of cash and goodies I guess he tossed me an easy $100,000 over fifteen years.

Did I invest in real estate or the futures market? Did I take an option on Telstra shares? No. It all went on buying guns and fighting blood wars in and out of prison.

It wasn't a lot of money but my crew had the full use of cars and properties, homes, flats and massage parlours owned or controlled by Rand and while in prison I'd spend about a hundred dollars per week on food. I had a five-grand-a-year food bill all paid for by Peter and if you count how many years' jail I did, you can see you it added up.

Any of my crew or men associated with me could see Peter for a sling. When Mad Charlie got out of prison in the early 1980s Peter Rand slung him $25,000 and placed him in charge of a massage parlour until I told Peter to withdraw all help because of Charlie's friendship with Alphonse.

So, all in all, Peter Rand turned out to be a lovely old lady to have on side. He really was my fairy godmother over the years.

Why a person like Peter was so fascinated with a world he was so clearly not part of is a psychological question I am unable to answer, but he was my financial backing in hard times off and on for at least fifteen to twenty years.

I had the use of his cars, his boat, his holiday home in Sorrento and the use of his bank book all because I stood between him and the world he was so fascinated with – and prevented that world from eating him up. I was his insurance policy and he was my financial pink security blanket.

He was a strange friend for me to have and I guess I was an even stranger friend for him to have. It was more than just business, I really did like him.

Ah well, the old girl is gone now. *Ivia con dios Signoretta*.

ANNA MARTIN (not her real name) was only a young teenage girl when she first met Chris Flannery at Micky's disco in St Kilda. She was little more than a kid, and I could only guess at her age. She was sitting at the bar and announcing in a loud voice that she had never met a man she couldn't deep throat, thus gaining the full attention of every man in the club.

I didn't see her again until 1987, about ten years later. She was still only knee high to a grasshopper, but a very well-put together lass with a very cheeky face and a knowing smile.

'How's it going, Chopper?' she said. It was going all right and going to get better, I thought.

I was standing in the Chevron nightclub and looked down at a set of big smiling eyes and a wide-mouth grin. All tits and legs in a micro mini and stiletto high heels.

'You don't remember me, do you?' she said. I didn't reply.

'Suzie,' she said. I still didn't reply. I was pretty cool back then.

'Suzie Blue,' she said. I shook my head.

'Vicki?' she said again.

I still didn't remember her. Suzie, Vicki, how many names did this scallywag have? Then she stood on the tiptoes of her stilettos and whispered into my missing left ear, the ear that matches my missing right ear.

'I've never met a man that I couldn't deep throat,' she whispered. 'Remember Micky's Disco?'

My brain woke up. So did something else. 'Anna Martin,' I said.

'Yeah.' She smiled.

The music was a bit loud so I yelled, 'That's ten years ago. You got a good memory considering we didn't know each other then and we don't know each other now, and you never took your knickers off for me.'

I always had the gift of the gab.

She was a bit taken aback, but continued on. 'I know you by reputation and I know you were there that night.'

I thought I knew her by reputation also. I was a gunnie and she was a gummy, if you know what I mean.

'So what are you doing these days?' I asked.

'You mean who am I doing, don't you?' She giggled.

I smiled back. She was such a wag.

I was waiting for Mad Charlie. He was in the piano bar talking with Athol. Athol ran the Chevron back then. There were darkened parts of the Chevron where a gentleman could take a lady, but I'd rather use Athol's office.

'Yeah, well, who are you doing?' I asked.

'Mad Charlie,' replied Anna.

The reason for her talking to me now clicked in. She must have known I was with Charlie. I relaxed and forgot all ideas of taking Anna to some dark and private area within the club.

'How long you known Charlie?' I asked.

'A few years,' she replied.

I nodded. I was losing interest fast.

'Big Al introduced us,' she continued.

I regained my interest. 'Al who?' I asked.

'Alphonse Gangitano,' she said as if I had just come from Mars. I just nodded.

'If you want to know about a bloke then talk to the chick who's got him by the dick,' I thought to myself.

'You got a phone number?' I asked. Anna nodded and handed me her business card. She seemed as eager to talk to me as I was to talk to her.

Charlie arrived with Athol and I talked to Athol while Mad Charlie removed Anna to a more private and darkened area of the club. As she walked away with Charlie she looked back over her shoulder at me and gave me a wide smile and a cheeky wink. I smiled and nodded back.

I let the matter rest for a week or so then rang Anna and arranged to meet her at a hotel in Collingwood, the one area neither Alphonse nor Mad Charlie would venture into. We met at the Leinster Arms Hotel in Gold Street. I've written about the Leinster Arms Hotel before in my crime-fiction books. It is one of the great old back-street Collingwood pubs that few people know of outside of Collingwood.

While Anna Martin isn't her real name, her real name isn't necessary for this story. Girls like her go under many different names. They have names they dance under, names to shag under when they work in the parlours, and years later, if they're not dead from drugs or a bullet, they change their names when they get married and pump out a few kids.

Anna did work under other names back then – Vicki and Suzie were two of them. Anna worked in the prostitution game, turning her hobby into a job. She was no fool and set up and ran parlours for other people: training new girls, setting up escort services and brothels. She was either upper management or the best French polisher in the business, depending on what paid best at that time. She had a solid gold American Express card for an arse.

She was a money-making machine. She didn't use drugs, she wasn't some mindless gangster moll, junkie gutter slut. She was just a girl ducking and diving her way through the chessboard of life in an industry peppered with blood and betrayal. Her idea being to screw her way through the valley of the shadow of death and come out the other end, rich and very much alive.

In the 1980s death and injury wasn't totally unheard of. I quite liked Anna Martin. She was a smart chick with a heap of dash.

WE met around midday and she beat me at pool at $20 a game until I'd handed over about $100. She chatted about Charlie and Alphonse and seemed to know phone numbers, names and addresses that I needed to know.

She was a great help in relation to all sorts of information that I desperately needed. I'd been in Pentridge for the past nine and a half years and the several hours I spent with her that afternoon proved very important. Who was up who, movements of people, who were allies and who were enemies, pillow talk to the girls about different criminal liaisons. It was the sort of information that could save your life and cost someone else theirs.

But why was she telling me all this? Was she setting me up? I kept asking myself why Anna was being so helpful, but I knew that if I didn't ask she would end up telling me.

'Is it true?' asked Anna, 'that you nearly killed Shane Goodfellow in H Division, Pentridge?' I nodded.

Anna continued, 'Goodfellow and his mates pack-raped me a few years ago. I mean they nearly killed me. I see him with Alphonse all the time but what can I do? I have to smile and pretend it never happened, but it did happen, Chopper, and I don't forget and I don't forgive,' said Anna.

Suddenly I realised that little Anna was a lady with a serious score to settle and a long memory.

'Are you still polishing that dog Alphonse?' I asked.

'I polish a lot of guys, Chopper. It don't mean I like 'em. You know Mad Charlie is going to set you up for Alphonse?' she said.

'How do you know this?' I asked. She smiled.

'Al likes to big note himself. You would be amazed the shit he tells me while I'm jumping up and down on his dick.'

I stopped playing pool and sat down. She sat next to me.

'You know, I reckon you're gonna be a good little mate to have on side, Princess,' I said.

'That's what I was thinking,' replied Anna.

I walked away from the Leinster Arms Hotel that day with a new friend and, no, I didn't get into her pants. That's one of the reasons we stuck so staunch: I was probably the only bloke who hadn't tried to get up her since she was thirteen. The enemy of my enemy is my friend.

Because of her warning I was able to keep my guard up with Charlie. If she hadn't I probably would have been led to my death by a man I considered my mate. I'm still close friends with Anna to this day and remembering that both Alphonse and Mad Charlie are dead, murders that I believe will never be solved, regardless of what the police and media may believe, I will simply leave the readers to ponder the heart-warming story of Anna Martin.

I may make mention of her as I go along, but in relation to Alphonse and Mad Charlie and even the late Shane Goodfellow, I will depart the topic by simply saying, what better friend to have than a friend who is, to put it politely, sleeping with the enemy?

I will leave the Anna Martin story with her favourite quote by American Country singer Jeanie Seely: 'I woke up on the right side of the wrong bed this morning.'

CHAPTER 4

NOT THE AVON LADY

'It was almost as if someone was working their way down a list ... you'd have to know the rank structure to know who was going to be next.'

IT WAS very early in the morning of 9 January 1999, and the phone rang. It was a reporter asking me what I knew about Vincenzo Mannella. Poor Vinnie had been gunned down in his driveway in North Fitzroy. Apart from explaining the whole structure of the Italian-Australian criminal world, all I could say without getting myself involved was that Vinnie had been a small-time crim and a big-time gambler who lost more than he won.

He had also been a mate of the late Alphonse Gangitano. None of these things were going to be good for his health, especially all at once.

My opinion isn't evidence so the reporter didn't repeat it and I won't repeat it now. Given the Flannery fiasco, it is clear that my opinion is considered evidence in some quarters. What I will say is that Vinnie was a forty-eight-year-old knockabout hood who also liked to shroud himself in the Mafia myth. He was also a sort of mate with the late Mad Charlie, who got his lights put out a few months beforehand in his front yard in Caulfield. Big Al, Mad Charlie and Vincenzo Mannella all got whacked in their own homes or outside their own homes by a man lying in wait or a visitor to the home under the cover of darkness, and all three knew each other.

Naturally the police and media see no link at all. Why should they? After all, the wood is impossible to see because there are too many bloody trees in the way.

I would go as far as to say all three men had known each other for a good twenty years, had played cards together till the wee hours of many a morning, had drunk at the same clubs together all night long, for a long, long time, and probably shared the same whores or whore over a stretch of years.

They were as friendly as three men could be in a world where no man really trusts the other. It was almost as if someone was working their way down a list and you'd have to know the rank structure to know who was going to be next. But then again, what would I know? I'm just a middle-aged, fat, has-been chicken farmer, so I will leave it all to the great crime solvers.

I sleep safe in my bed at night knowing that such crime solvers are awake and out there on the job. Poor old Chopper Read, he is so far behind he can't hear the band playing. But when the wind blows from the mainland and all is quiet in Tassie, you can just hear The Munster laughing, or is he coughing?

MY old H Division, Pentridge enemy Keith Faure paid me a surprise visit a while ago. I was dipping sheep about a half a mile away when he called. I saw these two people, a man and a woman, driving down the mile-long dirt driveway on the property next to ours. I thought they were a pair of God botherers as we get a few bible-bashing door knockers round this way. I went up to the pub to find a letter waiting for me. I'd sent Keith a Christmas card and he had come down to see me forgetting that us farmers are hard to find. His letter read as follows:

'Dear Mark,

Missed you, I called in as a surprise, I really am disappointed that I didn't see your crazy face. I came with my lady for a brief tour of Tasmania. She, too, looked forward to meeting you. I called at your place. Your lady, a little despondent, however understandable. Will catch up with you later on perhaps. Thank you for the Xmas card, sentiments expressed are a mutual embrace of my idealism also. Take care Mark, all the best. We regret nothing as you said. Let the rats walk the hard roads of ours. See how long they last. Buona fortune.

– Keith Faure, Richmond Arms 10.1.99.'

I bet my wife was despondent. The mad buggers had asked for Mark Brandon Read at three different farms in the area. Anyone asking for me gets told nothing. Farm people don't hand out information freely and the poor lady on the other property shit herself when they asked, 'Is Mark home?' Within an hour the whole Richmond district knew of the visit of two strangers looking for me. Had Keithy thought to tell anyone his last name I would have stopped dipping sheep and headed for the pub for a drink as I hold no ill will toward Keithy.

We both did what we had to do back then. Why Keithy introduced himself to people as Keith from Hobart is beyond me. When I heard Keith from Hobart was looking for me I said I only know two Keiths, my dad and Keithy Faure, and neither come from bloody Hobart. The next time you come to visit, Keithy, for Christ's sake write me a bloody letter to the Richmond Post Office.

Now, where was I?

I'VE just got myself a video camera. I'm off to see Shane Farmer, the owner of the Men's Gallery nightclub in Hobart, to get Alison 'Candy' Downes on camera. I can see it now, a Chopper Read production, interview with a lap dancer.

Priests have been defrocked for waving at Candy from a distance of 300 yards. She is a dead-set weapon in the looks department but quite a normal, everyday girl when you talk to her, and a personal friend. Even my wife likes her. How many wives would allow their husbands to have Miss Nude Australia as a friend? It says volumes about Alison's personality and Mary-Ann's sound judgement.

Alison has seen more of the world than I ever will. She has danced from London to New York. Never dismiss the adventures girls get into. Some men tell a better yarn because they talk louder, but Candy has told me a few to put my stories to shame.

DANIEL 'Danny Boy' Mendoza was a strange sort of fellow when I first met him in 1987.

He had only been in Australia about seven or so years and didn't speak the best of English. He came from Romania and was introduced to me by the late Albanian crime boss Nayim 'Norm' Dardovski at the Builders Arms Hotel in Fitzroy.

'Romanian Danny' was into everything and was trying to import Russian prostitutes into Australia by arranging bogus marriages. The husband, generally a Romanian working for the Romanian crime gangs, was given about a hundred or a hundred and fifty dollars per week out of the earnings of the Russian whore who could make between a thousand and fifteen hundred dollars per night in a Romanian-controlled massage parlour or brothel. One hundred and eighty dollars per hour for an eight-to ten-hour shift, five to six nights per week.

The whore would pocket about a thousand or fifteen hundred of her own money per week that she could either save, spend or invest with her Romanian minders in the heroin and methamphetamine industries.

One whore could average five to seven thousand dollars a week so there was enough cash in it for the Russian whore and her Romanian protectors to be interested. One parlour or brothel working six ladies on the night shift and four on the day shift, we never close, rear entrance, parking available, so the advertisement read, was pulling in fifty to seventy thousand per week.

So it wasn't small change. These Russian girls were all big, strong, tall, well-built ladies, long legs, big tits, big hips, I mean they were very good-looking, voluptuous Amazons. And they never said *nyet*.

They spoke several languages except English. I met a few of these ladies. They all called me Mr Chopper, thinking Chopper was my real name. Danny Boy Mendoza – that wasn't his real name, Danny Boy or Danny was the name he was called by. He was also known as Romanian Danny – would check in on the various Russian girls under his control.

The point was they worked for the Romanians while maintaining the facade of a marriage. The trouble was their Romanian husbands sometimes demanded a larger slice of the pie or, horror of horrors, would fall in love and demand she stop working.

The husbands created all the problems. Danny's job was to see that the girls had no problem with their husbands. More cash could be arranged, two hundred even three to five hundred a week could be arranged, but sex between the Romanian husband and the whore Russian wife generally meant the simple Romanian silly enough to involve himself in this immigration scam was also silly enough to fall in love.

Later the Russian whore immigration scam came undone and backfired on the Romanians when the Russian wives began bringing out their own brothers, mothers, fathers, uncles and so on.

Suddenly the fucking Romanians found their Russian whores waving goodbye and the Romanians unable to move against the Russian relatives, most of whom were Russian criminals. It was a real mess. You wouldn't know whether to give it to the NCA or the UN. By the way, what is Romanian for blow job?

Danny Boy mixed in this world. Drug dealing, arms dealing, prostitution, immigration fraud, social-security fraud, extortion, blackmail. He was murdered in June, 1998, and no wonder.

It was rumoured to be on the orders of a Romanian crime boss nicknamed The Gypsy or the Young One. I won't mention his name. I knew him in Pentridge Prison in the late 1980s. He was doing four years for social-security fraud.

He was a very quiet and polite gentleman with the smile of a vampire and the look of a friendly undertaker. He knew old Norm the Albanian and we became friends as a result. So I wasn't bothered with his real name. Romanian names are so hard to remember anyway and my memory is fading.

Anyway, back to the story. Danny once took me to a brothel in Footscray he claimed he owned. Back then his name on introduction was Magdalin Dimitrou. I called him My Darlin' Danny Boy.

Magdalin sounded like 'my darlin'. He didn't like that but, oh well. He chatted about being in the Romanian Army and coming to Australia as a refugee, and the Russian girls under his control or in his charge. He was eager to impress old Norm via my good self. Danny owed old Norm money – $5,000. Now, there have been many people in the crime world who had inflated reputations as tough guys, but let me say that Norm was a man who was always given respect. He was a real hard man who didn't need headlines and hangers-on to create some gangster image.

I thought to myself then, if Danny was such a Romanian big shot how come he couldn't repay the loan?

It turned out Danny may have handled the girls but other Romanians handled the cash. Danny was only a bit player in a much larger production. We got to the brothel and Danny and I went inside. He introduced me to a Russian beauty queen nearly as tall as myself with a body that could hardly be contained under the satin dressing gown she was nearly wearing. The plan was for this Russian vacuum cleaner to suck my brains out, and as a result I would become Danny's best friend.

It seemed like a good plan to me. I couldn't fault it, really.

The Russian girl spoke almost no English except for, 'You like?'

Was that a trick question?

'Yes,' I replied, 'I like.'

'You have wife?'

'No,' I replied, 'no wife.'

She understood the no wife bit and went at it like a mad woman. I had my pants down around my ankles with my roll of money in my left hand and my gun in my right hand. She was on her knees with both hands grabbing my tattooed bum and her mouth around the rest of me coming up for air long enough to ask some stupid broken English question.

She clearly didn't know that in refined company it was rude to speak with one's mouth full.

'You Danny's friend?'

'Yes, I'm Danny's friend.'

'You no pay money, I do coz I like you,' she said.

'Yeah,' I thought, 'I've heard that before'.

'I see you again?'

'Yeah, you see me again.'

'My name Yousna, your name Choppa?'

'Yeah, my name Chopper'.

OK, so it wasn't riveting dialogue, but we were both kinda busy.

'You have phone number?'

'No, I don't.'

'I give you mine,' she said. God knows where she intended to write it.

'Yeah, OK,' I said.

Then back to work she went. She was no slacker, that's for sure.

Later we went back to the lounge room waiting area and Yousna gave Danny a big kiss on the mouth.

Yousna then turned to me and put out her hand and I shook it solemnly as though we were business colleagues.

'I see you, Choppa, you nice man, you ring me?'

And with that she gave me her phone number.

'You want see me you ring.' It was more an order than a question.

'Yeah, I'll ring,' I said and with a wave I walked out. Danny, wanting to big note himself, grabbed Yousna on the arse and put his face between her big tits and proceeded to blow imaginary bubbles. He was such a card.

She giggled and that was that. Two hours later, as a favour to old Norm, I've got a gun in Danny's mouth telling him he had till tomorrow to repay the five grand. Blowing bubbles indeed.

That night in the bar of the Builders Arms Hotel in Fitzroy, Yousna walks in looking for me. I didn't flatter myself that she was in love. Not when old Norm recognised her as Danny Boy's live-in girlfriend. I took Yousna to meet Mad Charlie and she entertained Mad Charlie, myself and assorted other members of Charlie's crew. Charlie was talking to her in wog talk. I couldn't understand a word. The next thing I know is she is in tears and Charlie is taking me into the hallway for a private talk.

'What's going on?' asks Charlie.

I acted dumb.

'What's going on with you and her boyfriend?'

'He owes old Norm five grand.'

'I told you to stay away from them fucking Albanians,' screams Mad Charlie.

'Who are you talking to, you bald-headed dwarf?' I yelled back.

'Jesus, Charlie,' I continued, 'you can't help yourself. You spend half an hour up her arse and now you wanna give me the arse.'

'Fuck Norm,' said Charlie, 'let the old dog collect his own money.'

'There's the telephone, Charlie,' I said. 'Ring Norm up and tell him your fuckin' self.'

Mad Charlie may have been mad but he wasn't crazy. Norm was not a man to phone with obscenities. He turned and just walked away.

Yousna had found a new friend and through Yousna Mad Charlie started doing business with Danny and the Romanians and Norm got his five grand back. I saw Yousna about a month later with Mad

Charlie and Danny. She saw me and ignored me, a real nose in the air job.

She was no longer working in brothels and had become Mad Charlie's personal private dirty girl while still living with Danny. I believe she died of a heroin overdose about a year later in a brothel in Carlton after both Mad Charlie and Danny Boy had dumped her.

The point of the story being Danny Mendoza and his Russian whore girlfriend were the ones who introduced Mad Charlie to the Romanian criminal world. Every crime story generally involves a girl and they are generally left out of every story. I try not to do that. After all, fair's fair.

CHAPTER 5

HOW LOOSE LIPS STARTED A WAR

'Cash of up to a million or two changed hands at the Melbourne Cup, but that arrangement vanished shortly after the bookie job went off. Just as well, because they were next.'

IT is often said that wisdom comes from the mouths of babes and I guess the most profound remark made to me in recent times came from the mouth of a babe. Alison Downes (aka Candy) sat in the kitchen of her pub in Hobart eating an apple. She made Eve look like some fat slag in a brunch coat.

I was watching TV with her business partner, who could also be her boyfriend and/or husband. I don't quite know their personal arrangements and I am too polite to ask. In the old days I used to be more curious about people's situations and I would often enquire of Melbourne drug dealers concerning their financial arrangements, although it would be difficult to hear their answers when I was wearing a welder's mask and they invariably mumbled due to a pair of socks stuffed in the mouth.

But I digress. I've known Shane Farmer since his time at the Chevron nightclub in Melbourne in the 1970s and he was a seriously wild man. How he ended up in the company of Alison all these years later had me stuffed, and her too, probably. Alison munched away at her apple and said, 'You know, Chopper, all you have really done is to make the best of your situation.' I thought about that remark then looked back at Alison who was sitting on the couch trying to tuck the longest legs I'd ever seen since I can't remember when up under her chin while munching on fruit. Oh, she just banged her chin on her own kneecap while chewing on a Jonathan.

'What did you just say, Ally?' I asked.

'I said, all you have really done, Chopper, is you've made the best of your situation and that's all any of us can do really, isn't it?'

I nodded, not wanting to let her know that it was probably the most downright profound comment I'd heard in a long while. Imagine, a philosopher with a chest that was beyond belief.

You spend your time looking at strippers, not knowing that some of them are looking back.

She was right, of course, we all just try to do the best with what we've got. Alison was drop-dead gorgeous so she gets paid a truck-load of money to let people look at her. If she didn't blokes would still perve at her, except they wouldn't pay.

We all try to make the best of every Vesta situation.

I guess that's all Norm Lee ever did. The Great Bookie Robbery dim sim money man. I should say the late Norm Lee – and not because he had a broken watch. All he ever did was to make the best of his situation.

Like Romanian Danny, Norm was only a bit player in a much bigger production. He just happened to live a wee bit longer than most of the other bit-part players. Norm is dead, but before he died, he big-noted himself to various people, including his lawyer Phillip Dunn QC, that he, Norman Lee, was part of the actual six-man team that carried out the Great Bookie raid.

I know that what the police and the media believe becomes folklore and is believed to be the truth, and my opinion will fly in the face of that folklore, but this is my opinion. Believe it or bash it up your bum. I couldn't give a shit, but I did time with these blokes so I reckon I can have my say.

I won't spend much time on this as, like the Flannery matter, it is yesterday's news for me, but I think it is worthwhile getting history down in the interest of accuracy. Otherwise half the crap that has been spoken about crime will be regarded as fact in a few years. Maybe Ned Kelly was just an idiot with a good publicist, who knows now?

Now settle down, pull the blanket up to your chin and let Professor Manning Chopper give you a quick history lesson.

Remember the name Marko M ... and if it's not mentioned by anyone claiming to know the truth of the Great Bookie Robbery, then the person telling the story has been told a lie.

I knew Marko and he was part of the six-man team. He had more sheer guts than all of 'em, bar Ray Chuck himself. Who else told me that Marko was part of the six-man crew other than Raymond Patrick Chuck Bennett himself, not to mention Tony McNamara.

Both Tony and Ray were part of the team and they are no longer with us. But some of the team survive – one of them I shall only call Brian. He was the seventh man of the team but wasn't even at the Victoria Club when it all went down. He was in H Division, Pentridge when the job went off, but still got his cut. Another man on the team I will call Russell. Both these men confirmed their involvement in the job to me after they found out that I knew Marko and that I was a friend of both Ray Chuck's and Tony McNamara.

So now we have Ray Chuck, Tony McNamara, Russell and Brian the seventh man. So that's three of the six who went through the door. Marko M makes four. Marko went back to Yugoslavia after the job and has never been heard of since. He may return either to kill me or sue me, but I doubt it.

It was Mad Charlie who introduced me to Marko; there weren't many Yugoslav criminals Charlie didn't know. Oh, by the way, the two remaining names are Jimmy 'Jockey' Smith and Ian Revel Carroll. Leslie Kane, Brian Kane and Laurie Prendergast had little to do with it. They came in after the event as part of an ongoing war between the Kanes and Ray Chuck.

As for Norm Lee, he was Ray Chuck's 'dog's body' helper and gofer and never part of the six-man crew. There was one other name I should mention – Stan James who, like so many of that time, is now dead. When I mentioned to Tony McNamara the Ian Carroll story (as told to me by Ray Chuck) Tony smiled and said, 'You don't expect Chuckles to tell you all the truth, do you, Chopper?'

It was then that he tossed in the Stan James story. Whatever the truth, I'm sure I've named the whole crew without fully naming the two still-living members – Brian and Russell, who may want to come down to Tassie for a chicken dinner.

Careful readers who can add up will note that Stan James makes a list of seven – Ray, Tony, Russell, Marko, Jockey, Ian and Stan – of which six went through the door, with Brian not able to get to the church due to a previous engagement with a prison cell. And the real figure was six and a half million dollars.

Remember the name Marko M. A clue: his surname sounds like a cross between a mountain and a trick. His name is the key; anybody who doesn't know it in relation to the bookie robbery is talking shit. Anyway, what do I care? I never got any dough out of it even though I later ended up with one of the Owen machine guns used in the robbery. The funny thing is, the slide bolt on the Owen was seized up and had been for at least ten years, which means that at least one of the six machine guns used in the robbery didn't even bloody work.

Hardly matters though, does it? A gang of bookies on the port wine eating stilton cheese in the Victoria Club were hardly going to overpower the gang even if they had only been armed with tuning forks. Half the money was black, so what were they going to do any rate?

I will say, however, that having known three members of the six-man team very well and the other three fairly well you could write what they all knew about firearms on the back of a postage stamp.

In other words, the Owen gun with the rusted and seized-up slide bolt didn't surprise me. It only took two hours to fix but no one in that crew knew how. I was dumbfounded but I won't bag them over it. They got the cash and I got the old gun, so who was the dummy?

I was given the seized-up Owen gun in 1977 without ammo. So, you clever scallywags may well ask, how do I know it was used in the robbery? Well, smart Alecs, Marko dropped it off for me at my dad's place before he left Australia so I think it's safe to put two and two together and come up with four. Or even six and half million.

I could be wrong but I doubt it. Like the Flannery story, it's my opinion – and you can believe it or bash it up your arse. You've already bought the book and no doubt you've probably spilled Milo on it so you can't take it back. Take it up with the bimbo behind the counter at the bookshop.

FOR almost a hundred years the bookies of Melbourne met at the old Victoria Club at 141 Queen Street to settle up on the first day of business after a big weekend metropolitan race meeting. The biggest movers in the racing world in Victoria turned up there to whack up the take. The system had stood the test of time, and no one took much notice of it. But the fact was that vast sums of cash arrived on settling day by armoured car – however, once inside the club there was almost no security at all. More a matter of habit than common sense.

A similar set-up went on at the Melbourne Club between grand old gents with knighthoods and political titles. In private betting arrangements, cash of up to a million or two changed hands but that arrangement vanished shortly after the bookie job went off. Just as well, because they were next on the list.

Everything worked on trust and the bookies all worked on trust. This in itself was insane, as it was an old bookie who first put the idea to an old member of the Victorian Federated Ship Painters and Dockers Union as a nice little earner. The nearest thing to security was that the old Victorian Police Consorting Squad had an informal arrangement to pop into the Victoria Club for a drink on settling day. If you knew the old Consorters you would know that was no surprise. They were known to pop in for a free drink just about everywhere in Melbourne. I think they invented the drink card.

The story of the bookie robbery has been told and retold until it's almost become a fairytale. A Melbourne bedtime story with a twist in the tale. The twist was, for those who don't know, that it just so happened that the consorting crew didn't show up on this particular day.

The cash from 116 bookies was delivered by Mayne Nickless armoured truck at seven minutes past midday on 21 April 1976. Ray Chuck and the crew hit. Thirty-one people were ordered to lie on the floor, one smart guard went for his .38 revolver and got belted with the butt of a machine gun. Ray Chuck did that. The two phones were pulled out and the eight Mayne Nickless cash boxes cut open with bolt cutters. A hundred and eighteen cash bags were removed and stuffed into seamen's duffle bags. Three duffle bags in all. One man raised his head to see what was going on. Ray Chuck yelled out, 'On the floor, hit the fuckin' deck, everyone down!' But old Ambrose Palmer, the famous boxing trainer who took Johnny Famechon to a world title, raised his head to see what was going on and one of the bandits yelled out, 'You too, Ambrose.' Old Ambrose had known Tony 'Veggie' McNamara since he was a young kid and Ambrose recognised Tony's voice. Old Ambrose stuck staunch and said nothing to the law but confided in a few people close to him that the words 'You too, Ambrose' were uttered by Tony.

Well, if you confide in one you confide in a million and the word soon got out – not to the police but to the Kane brothers, which was probably worse in the long run. The Kanes knew Palmer and while the grand old man of boxing had kept his mouth shut to the police he had unknowingly started a gang war that would see the Melbourne underworld torn in half.

'You too, Ambrose.' Three little words that brought the biggest job in Aussie history undone and cost the lives of almost every man involved. What not many people know is that Tony knew straight away that Ambrose had recognised his voice. As they drove away with millions in three bags Tony wasn't smiling. He felt sick. So sick, in fact, that Ray Chuck thought Tony was suffering some sort of aftershock.

'What could I do?' Tony explained to me later. 'Tell Chuckles what I knew, and Ambrose would have been shot to death next day.' Tony was a thief, not a killer.

Then again, what would I know? I'm just the fat farmer in the white T-shirt. Believe it or bash it up your bum. I don't care. You could check with Tony but you'd have to do it with a psychic because that's the only way he'll be answering the phone.

Fact is, Anthony Paul McNamara died of a heroin overdose at a house in Easey Street, Collingwood, in 1990. I spoke to the Veggie shortly before his death. It seems his address book with my name and address and phone number in it, my dad's address and phone number and other personal details relating to me fell from his pocket. The two blokes he was with stopped and one picked it up and handed it to Tony.

As luck would have it, the book had fallen open at the spot where my name was written. Not much was said. Not much needed to be said. I'd shot both the chaps he was with in the guts many years earlier. Tony said he wasn't concerned but, for a bloke who reckoned he wasn't concerned, he went to some bother to contact me over the fallen address-book matter.

I was in H Division, Pentridge at the time. I'm not saying one thing related to the other but it wasn't the first time mates of mine had paid the price for running with two crews at the same time. In Melbourne there can be no shades of grey, only black and white. A lot of people I knew from those days are now maggot mulch.

The lies told by cops and robbers are legend. Sometimes it is better all round for the public to believe the myths while the truth remains hidden forever. I guess I've been as guilty of this as anyone else in the real know. If a fairytale, folklore yarn is told for long enough then it becomes truth and a good bloke can walk off into the sunset of life a free man. I reckon anyone silly enough not to be able to work it out for themselves deserves to be told a lie. For example, who shot Ray Chuck inside the old Melbourne magistrates court building in 1979 will never be known for sure. But if so-and-so really did Ray Chuck then you'd need to be almost mentally retarded not to work out who did so-and-so. And if I can help keep a good bloke from a life sentence then so be it.

If you're quick on the uptake and able to read between the lines the truth threads its way in and out of every yarn.

It's like the bloke who is writing this book. He has got ears … you just can't see them.

CHAPTER 6

A DEAD MAN CALLING

'Charlie hung up. I knew he was in serious trouble, I just didn't know if he realised how deep.'

IT is 8 April. My wife Mary-Ann's birthday. Yesterday I went to Hobart to buy her a birthday gift but I ended up at Shane Farmer's and Alison Downes's nightclub, The Men's Gallery in Hobart. Now, I thought they might have some nice bath crystals or a box of Quality Street chocolates there but I was hijacked by firewater and naughty girlies.

Evidently I got rotten drunk and was putting my head between the dancers' legs and giving them shoulder rides round the club against their will, I'm told.

I thought it was the height of good humour, but I may have been wrong. I was being rude to American sailors, singing a song called, 'Cotton Fields' to a group of black gentleman and generally making an arsehole of myself.

You must remember I was in prison when political correctness crept up on the outside world, which makes me a member of some sort of deprived minority, when you think about it.

The bouncer asked me to tone it down. I told him to come back when he had learnt how to fight. He left without further comment. I thought he may cry. Funny, that. One lady ended up in tears after proudly showing me her brand-new boob-enlargement job. Most impressive. I advised her to go back and get her face fixed as a job lot. Ha, ha. Who said stand-up is dead?

I ran up a bar bill of several hundred dollars. I was only drinking scotch and cokes but at eight to nine per hour for six hours plus food I suspect someone had been playing with the book keeping. My wife was called and she came in and took me home – and, you guessed it, I forgot her birthday gift. Mary-Ann told me I'm an alcoholic. With that sort of rap I could have been Prime Minister.

I said, 'I don't hit you and your purse is always full so what's the problem?' Then she said she doesn't want little Charlie to be brought up by a drunk.

Bingo, that hit home. Oh, I forgot to mention that, at the time of writing, Mary-Ann is going to have a baby. I told her that we will have to go to the doctor and find out what caused it, then we must stop doing it right away.

It is going to be a boy from the scan and I'm naming him Charles Vincent Read. Charles after Mad Charlie because the baby was conceived on or around the time Mad Charlie got put off and Vincent after old Vincent Villeroy and my father-in-law, Ernest Vincent Hodge.

I do enjoy a social drink and if I am an alcoholic I'm a bloody friendly, happy one, but I may have to tone down my drinking as Mary-Ann's remark hurt. The remarks of wives are meant to hurt and they seem to know what to say and the right or wrong time to say it as well.

IT is 5.30am as I write this. I must let my chickens out and feed them and start my general duties on the farm. Paul Manning and I cut several tons of wood the other day and I think we have some other nice jobs lined up for today. It's either dipping sheep, drenching sheep, crutching sheep or shearing fucking sheep or bloody ploughing up the paddocks with the tractor. And to think I spent years fighting to get out of jail, to do this.

It's all good fun. Carting hay is a great job. Eight or nine hours flat out in the sun tossing bales of hay on to the back of a trailer then unloading it and stacking it. Isn't it any wonder that I sometimes take a cool drink on a warm day and on occasions flee from the midday sun to head for the Men's Gallery?

Slip, slop, slap has been my motto. Slip on your shoes, slop some Irish whisky into ya, and slap some lap-dancer on the arse. No chance of skin cancer there.

The film people rang again. They live in another world, them sort of people. The Chinese built the bloody Great Wall in about the same time as this thing has been going on.

Anyway, back to the main event. At the time of writing the American war ship the USS *Carl Vinson* is in Hobart and half the knob polishers in Australia are here for the visit.

So far half the American sailors I've bumped into are as camp as a row of tents so a lot of girls are in for a shock unless they brought their brothers with them, and in Tassie they just could have.

I understand the world less and less. Sometimes it looks clearer through the bottom of a glass. Here we supposedly have one of the finest military forces in the world and I suspect they would be better off being armed with handbags.

When I was in school in the first grade the teacher told me one and one was two. 'Now, wait a minute,' I said, 'how do you know?' And right then we had our first big problem.

In reality how do any of us know anything for sure? Just because it's meant to be so, don't make it so. So when I write about Flannery, Alphonse, Mendoza, Mad Charlie, Vinnie Mannella, Ray Chuck, remember that. Just because what was meant to be, doesn't make it so. I knew these people through the years, some of them nearly all my life.

The myths, rumours, legends and stories relating to their lives and their deaths are in a large part created by people who didn't know them at all. The journos and the coppers who spoke of them and wrote about them with such knowledge wouldn't actually recognise them face to face, unless they served them a caffe latte in a sushi bar.

So, just remember that, while the men who pooh-pooh my version of events and opinions tell you I'm wrong and laugh at me and continue to weave these myths for you, I knew these blokes, no matter how many so-called keep telling you I'm wrong.

They never knew any of these blokes at all. I've got the scars to prove my CV. The only scars some journos have is from grabbing their glass of hot coffee without using a napkin. The most dash most of them show is not tipping a slow waiter.

Back to Mad Charlie. The last time I spoke to Charlie was on the telephone about a week before he died. It was 17, November 1998, my birthday. I pondered how he got hold of my unlisted phone number but I had learnt many years earlier never to wonder too long how Charlie got his info.

Our last conversation was light. 'How's it going, Chop?'

'What do you want, wog?'

'Happy birthday, mate.'

'Who gave you my phone number? Longley?' *(Editor's note: Billy 'The Texan' Longley, the former painter and docker, gunman and ballroom dancer.)*

'Nah,' said Charlie. 'Fuck Longley. Anyway, do you still talk to that old maggot?'

'Nah,' I said, 'I fell out with him over that shit with Jasmine and Maltese Dave.' This refers to a private matter that doesn't concern the readers who are not painters and dockers.

'You heard from Neville lately, Chop?' By this he meant Norm the Albanian's son.

'No, Charlie. But I've got his brother Richard's phone number,' I said.

'I need to talk to him,' said Charlie.

'How's the Greek going, mate?' I asked politely. Meaning Nick the Greek Apostolidis.

'I don't see him no more,' said Charlie, which I knew was a lie.

'What's wrong, mate, you don't sound too good? Are you still on the gear?' Meaning heroin.

'Who told you that?' said Charlie.

'The Jew,' I replied. 'Ah, fuck that mad cunt,' said Charlie. 'Keep him away from me.'

'So what's the problem, Charlie? Do you miss me now that Alphonse is gone? Ha ha.'

'Fuck Alphonse,' replied Charlie. 'Fuck 'em all. How come we fell out, Chop?'

'I don't know, Charlie, you tell me.'

'Yeah, well,' replied Charlie, 'fault on both sides.'

'Yeah,' I said, 'yours and yours. You took that dago's side against me and now you're all a fucking lone. Do you miss me a bit, Charlie?'

'Don't rub it in, no ears,' said Charlie.

'Are you still seeing Jandie?' I asked.

'Nah, who was that other one?' said Charlie, rattling off a list of girls' names.

'Suzie,' I said.

'Anna,' replied Charlie. 'Yeah, now and again. You married now?'

'Yeah,' I said.

'Me too,' said Charlie.

'You a father, I hear, Charlie.'

'Yeah, two kids. When are you coming back to Melbourne, mate?' asked Charlie.

'I don't know,' I said.

'We should see each other,' said Charlie.

'Yeah, OK Charlie,' I said. 'What's wrong, Charlie? I asked again.

'Ahh, you know,' said Charlie. 'More of the same old shit, only twice as much. I'll be right, I've fucked 'em before, I'll fuck 'em again.'

More conversation re phone numbers and personal details, then Charlie hung up. I knew he was in serious trouble, I just didn't know if he realised how deep.

The truth was Charlie had lost his army. When the barman calls last orders, you leave. Charlie refused to leave. I looked up an old phone number and rang Anna Martin.

She was now in her thirties and still looked in her twenties, I'm told.

She always thanked me for fixing her problem with Shane Goodfellow, somehow thinking I had a hand in his death, which I did not.

And because I predicted the death of Alphonse she, like a lot of others, thought I had a role to play in that as well. Which I did not.

Anna had been screwing Alphonse almost up to the moment he died. She was now working part time in a brothel in Collingwood. I rang her and asked her about Charlie. Sure enough, she was still seeing Charlie. Only he had been a bit sad the last few weeks, she said.

'Anna, Anna, Anna, what the fuck am I gonna do?' Charlie would moan.

'Do about what Charlie?' Anna would ask.

'Ahh, you know,' Charlie would reply, but Anna didn't know.

Anna was a Blow Queen and Charlie loved her doing the business. When Charlie was full of meth amphetamine speed this could last three to four hours at $250 to $300 per hour.

Charlie would sling Anna a flat grand whenever he called in, but lately he couldn't even get his dick stiff. Something was on his mind. He would sit in an armchair with his handgun resting beside him watching porno videos on TV with the sound turned down so he could listen to the late-night street noises, passing cars, footsteps and so on, relaxed, at ease, tired, yet paranoid and worried.

Anna would be on her knees between his legs desperately trying to blow life into something that didn't seem to be interested.

'What's wrong with him, Anna?' I asked.

'I know he misses you, Chop. He seems very lonely of late. I feel a bit sorry for him,' said Anna.

'I know a lot of the friends he did have he hasn't got no more.'

Anna and I chatted in general about life and this and that and the other and that was that. I even rang Dave the Jew about Charlie. All Dave could say is that Charlie was pretty much alone these days.

The new guys he mixed with weren't like the old crew. They would drink with him but not die with him.

He's all alone and feeling a bit sorry for himself. I felt a bit sad for Charlie myself after hearing all of that, but what could I do? Go back to Melbourne and hold his hand?

If I had done that I knew we would both die. I would bring trouble to him, not protect him from it. I'd held Charlie's hand for many years – for far too many years, some might say – and now it was up to Charlie to face his own demons all on his own. He was a general without an army. I felt sorry for Charlie, but Charlie always forgot that it was other people who put him where he was, and when those certain few people walked away from him he was finished. What happened had to happen. I'm surprised it took so long.

From this distance it was like watching something happen in slow motion.

Oh well.

CHAPTER 7

DANCING WITH DEATH

'The party was attended by sixty to eighty top Melbourne criminals. Off-duty police manned the door as security.'

A PAIR of long legs can walk through doors otherwise closed. A set of big tits and a pair of big eyes and an even bigger smile can float through the valley of the shadow of death like a butterfly. My long-legged blonde mate Alison Downes has won more Miss Nude and Miss Erotica contests than I've had Christmas dinners – and, please, no stuffing jokes here.

She has danced all over the world from New York, Las Vegas to London but would put the clubs in Melbourne up against the world's best with the exception of the clubs in Hawaii. When one sits and talks to a lap dancer who has worked the international dance circuit and done clubs, bars and private functions in New York and London, and hears stories about Italian stag parties in New York, one learns that there is a different world out there.

She doesn't brag, she just talks about things, like when she was in a posh London hotel – the Savoy, it was – for a turn put on for Arabs, who tossed fifty-pound notes on the floor until the carpet could no longer be seen while two strippers covered in baby oil rolled around the floor because whatever stuck to their skin they could keep.

Let's say if her chest got covered with fifty-pound notes she could pay off the national debt. One has to believe stories about parties in Melbourne put on by police and other parties put on by criminals when the lady telling the stories has danced on board visiting American warships and has walked, giggling, through doors marked High Security to put on strip shows for inmates in American Federal Prisons.

Then why should I disbelieve her when she tells me about a dancer she knew who danced for this group of people at this or that party or her own adventures dancing for various parties in Melbourne? So, without naming names, I will toss in a believe-it-or-not story about a bucks night in Melbourne about six months before Big Alphonse Gangitano got shot in 1997.

The party was held in the private area of a King Street club. A party attended by at least sixty to eighty top Melbourne criminals, including Alphonse and Mad Charlie. Off-duty police manned the door as security, which appealed to Big Al's sense of comedy.

A Lebanese criminal was getting married and a long blonde stripper was booked to put on the show. As she was getting changed and preparing to do the show she heard three gun shots, then one of the off-duty policemen came into the dressing room with two Italians and she was paid a thousand dollars and told the party was cancelled.

As she was being led out of the club she saw the Lebanese guest of honour lying on the floor in a pool of blood. Mad Charlie had a gun in his hand, so did Big Alphonse. She was bundled into a car and driven back to her motel room and told to lose her memory or she would lose her head.

She lost her memory at once and rather I not mention her name in this story. I listened to her yarn and she mentioned the names of a good dozen or so other men in attendance and I couldn't fault her or pick her up on any shaky detail, nor could I see why she would want to lie about such a thing.

Then I said I'd use the story in my ninth book and she asked me again not to mention her name for some reason. I believe her story to be true, believe it or not. I don't give a shit. I mentioned Alison Downes's name before but that doesn't mean that she was the dancer involved. However, I digress. Back to some more Mad Charlie stories.

OF all the criminals I could write about Charlie would be among the funniest, if not the funniest. People who try so hard to act in a serious manner tend to be quite comical.

I remember when Mad Charlie was a fifteen-year-old. He walked into the headquarters of the Victorian Federated Ship Painters and Dockers Union and asked the Big Boss, Doug Sproule, for a job. Sproule told Charlie to piss off. Now, in those days, the dockies ran Melbourne and Doug was a man not to be trifled with, so how did Charlie take his job application being rejected?

Mad Charlie yelled, 'Piss off yourself, you fat dog.' Doug Sproule came charging at young Charlie in rage. 'Who are you calling a dog you wog bastard?' he yelled.

Charlie spun around and aimed a .38 calibre handgun into Sproule's face. 'Back up, fat boy,' snarled Charlie. 'One day all you maggots will be working for me.'

It was an insane, comically true story about the fifteen-year- old kid who pulled the gun on Sproule after being knocked back for a job on the docks. A story told mostly by dockies to explain what a comical mental case Mad Charlie really was.

The funny part was, when drugs took total control of the Melbourne criminal world some ten years later, a great many painters and dockers did end up working for Mad Charlie, but Charlie was as cunning as he was mad. He was as mad as a rat and as cunning as a snake, or something like that.

Like the time he arranged for a crew to attack Brian, Les and Ray Kane outside a Melbourne nightclub so that Charlie could jump in and fight on the Kane brothers' side, thus appearing to save the day. All because he wanted to meet the Kane brothers. Couldn't he just drop them a note?

But that was Mad Charlie. He would do you a good turn to help you out of bad trouble and you would never know that it was Charlie who started all your trouble in the first place.

He would create the problem, then step in and solve it, receiving thanks and cash for doing so. Nice work if you could get it. Then when people started to view Charlie as the sly, cunning thinker that he really was he would pull a stunt to show one and all that he was a total nut job, just to keep them guessing.

Like the time he came to visit me in Bendigo prison with Nick the Greek Apostolidis in 1986. I was the one who introduced Apostolidis to Charlie in 1975. Why, I'll never know, but Charlie had used Apostolidis as a driver and general handy man ever since.

We were in the prison's contact visit area and something was said to Apostolidis by a friend of Graeme Jensen's. Graeme Jensen was also having a visit. Mad Charlie flew into a rage and wanted to fight Jensen in the visit yard then and there.

This was insane. Jensen shit himself. What mad man visits someone in prison then invites an inmate to partake in a fist fight in the bloody visit yard? Jensen couldn't believe it. He had to maintain face and pride while knowing that he had no chance of beating Mad Charlie having seen Charlie pull his coat back to reveal the butt of a small revolver tucked into his pants. Charlie had brought a handgun into a prison visit which tells you what sort of desperate we were dealing with. Metal detectors were not used to scan visitors in 1986 at Bendigo prison.

You don't have to be told. The whole thing was a staged event. I broke the would-be fight up, saving the day ... and stories of Charlie's madness were spread far and wide.

Charlie came to visit me with every intention of having a go at Jensen, a well-planned, calculated act of cunning madness. We can't ask Graeme what he thought about the whole charade, of course, because he's the same Graeme Jensen who lost the plot and half his head when he was shot dead by police at Narre Warren when he was illegally and feloniously in possession of a spark-plug for his motor-mower. Ha, ha.

ALPHONSE Gangitano would plan his acts of violence with the same cunning. Everything was controlled and planned to make Big Al look good. Mindless insanity such as I had become famous for had to be re-enacted without the risk of prison.

It was the stuff legends are made of. But, as a bloke who had been there and done it for real, it was easy for me to spot the staged events carried out by very sane men desperately trying to act crazy in a criminal world controlled by violent insanity.

It was at a time when the crazier you were the more dangerous you were and the more respect they had to give you. So crims pretended to be mad.

I didn't need to, back then.

The man in the grey suit brawl at the Sports Bar in King Street,

Melbourne was a staged event, as fake as a three-dollar bill. Gangitano, wearing a grey suit, and named in court and police statements as the man in the grey suit, cut loose in the Sports Bar with billiard cues and turned the club into a bloodbath. Big Al went to the club to collect money from the management then wrecked the place when the money was not forthcoming. It was all a staged event, put on to impress other club owners and criminals as well as onlooking prostitutes that Big Al was bigger and badder than ever in spite of the fact that he was touching middle age, touching the coke, and touching his own dick as well.

Prostitutes being the biggest gossips within the criminal structure, that two-bob nightclub brawl earnt him more brownie points then the shooting of Greg Workman.

Its easy to separate the real psychos from the false pretenders. Art imitates life and within the criminal world life can also imitate art. It is a stage full of actors. The separation of fact from fiction is almost impossible. Pretenders and role players walk hand in hand with true blue psychopaths.

The difference is that the real psychopath lives in a world all of his own, deep in his own mind. The psycho may very well enjoy the company of actors and role players provided that the psychopath can join in on a drama created by the play actors in a theatre funded by drug dollars.

The psychopath only wants to take part for his own comic reasons no matter if the game is true or false, created by real men or dream merchants. It is of no importance to the psychopath. He doesn't need to rehearse his lines in the play because he is not acting.

He doesn't care if the Alphonse Gangitanos and Mad Charlies of the criminal world are play acting at their own fantasy or serious hard men. All the psychopath wants is to be provided with a stage, a battlefield. Both Mad Charlie and Alphonse had psychopaths on their side but they both forgot that when the curtain comes down and the fat lady has sung her last song the psychopath will turn on the director and step over his body toward the next game and the next stage.

There you are, I've just told you who killed both men and why. Providing you know the name of each man's psychopath you can solve the riddle. Ha, ha.

But you'd already know the answer to that, wouldn't you? The police and media think they do, them being so smart and me being so stupid. Ha, ha. 'Ahh, Magoo, you've done it again.'

ATTILLA the Hen and Gloria Simpson have just had a massive fight in the barn yard. Attilla the Hen is really a rooster and much bigger than Gloria Simpson, but Gloria beat him.

Meanwhile, in all the excitement, Pauly the Parrot nearly bit the top of my left thumb off.

There are a family of possums living in the roof of our house and they come in through the kitchen window to raid the bread and jam.

Billy our dwarf Jack Russell barks his head off and the cats go mad but possums can outfight pound for pound any cat or dog. They can be quite vicious.

I've seen bull terriers and American Pit Bulls who have fought and killed a possum and it has always involved a large vet's bill for the owner of the dog.

The claws and teeth on a possum can rip the neck and guts out of a dog even while it is being savaged to death.

The possum will slash and rip and bite its final goodbye. Anyone who feels different has never sicked their dog on to a possum at night. Makes you wonder how the greyhound trainers give their dogs a 'kill' to get them keen. Once upon a time they would always pay you to trap them a possum or three for the dishlickers to get a taste of blood so the dimwitted bloody things would chase the lure. But I guess they used to muzzle the possums and blunt their claws first. Not what I call good sportsmanship. I'm sure it doesn't happen anymore, what with the RSPCA and everything. Even Tasmanian Devils who will attack and kill possums don't do so without injury. The possum is a much underestimated fighter and when I see one in my kitchen raiding the bread bin it looks at me as if to say 'Go on, have a go' and then moves on quietly.

I think to myself that I should look after my weight and the possums are doing me a favour in knocking off some of the jam. Plus I've already got enough scars from knives, baseball bats and bullets without being savaged by furry little cuddly animals.

They say the underworld is tough, but half the time out here in the great Australian bush I want to sleep under the bed with the blanket over my head.

Watchchook sleeps at night. If Watchchook was awake he'd have 'em. Who is Watchchook, you ask? My secret weapon.

Watchchook is a specially trained attack fowl fed on mince meat and is the dead-set, biggest, meanest most blood-crazy chicken God ever shovelled guts into.

Watchchook sleeps in a tree separate from the rest and will dive down on passers by. I tossed Watchchook up into a pine tree when he was a chick and fed him on mince meat, not grain like the other pansies.

It has sent Watchchook a bit silly. His tree is near the front gate and Watchchook is territorial and will swoop down screaming.

If you have ever been attacked from above and behind by a giant chicken then you'll know it can put you off your breakfast. You don't need a high-fibre diet to get the guts going when Watchchook tries to bungy jump on to your head.

When Watchchook attacks, the rest of the barn yard starts screaming, which means I can't be tiptoed up on during the day. I have another animal I let out at after dark to warn me of any night intruders but that, as they say in the classics, is another story. Ha, ha. Just as dangerous as Dave the Jew and less expensive to feed. Doesn't need any medication.

IT was 1974 and the parlour war, as the newspapers called it, was well and truly under way. Mad Charlie led the gang, and me, Mad Archie and Garry the Greek ran riot. We were having a great time. Prostitution was illegal, meaning massage parlours and brothels were operating against the law and the people who ran them, for the most part, were criminals who couldn't holler for the law.

Yes, millionaire businessmen like Peter the Poof controlled large chunks of the prostitution industry, but on a day-to-day level the girls and parlour managers and operators were all part of the criminal sub-culture.

They were good days. Telling on people was frowned on. Everyone knew each other. We would rob the parlours on a Friday night and be drinking with the girls on Saturday night.

We would walk in, smack the manager and bouncer minder about, rob the place and get our dicks sucked before the police were called and the girls promptly gave the police false descriptions of the offenders. Would have been a funny sort of line-up, eh.

I'd walk in and say 'come on girls, you know the drill' with a cheeky smile. By this time Mad Charlie was baseball batting the parlour minder and manager.

Any bloke in the place got a bat in the guts while all the girls got was a dick in the mouth. Our trick was we took the parlour money generally kept in some strong box in the kitchen or in the pocket of the manager.

We wouldn't take the girls' personal earnings. Most girls didn't like the hoons they worked for as they were often ripped off. The parlour owners, operators, managers and minders all thought that free sex was a perk of the job and the girls thought that putting a smile on our faces in one room while the parlour boss and/or minder screamed for mercy in the other room was quite comic.

The girls would tell us to hit a parlour at a certain time when the boss called in to collect the night's takings. I mean robbing a parlour blind without some inside knowledge meant you could hit a place for twenty dollars. A lot of parlours had floor safes.

We started off blind but our eyes soon opened. A parlour boss might smack a girl in the mouth for some nonsense to force her to have sex with one of his mates or a policeman for nothing.

She'd cop it sweet and do it – but if she saw us in a nightclub we'd have one more chick wanting us to rob her parlour and bash the heart and lungs out of the boss, the minder or her hoon pimp boyfriend. And, by the way, she'd say, you had better gang bang me as well just to make it look good.

Drag queens were the worst. If the parlour boss offended a drag queen she would go to the end of the earth to get her revenge. There was this one dark New Zealand drag queen transsexual, I never knew her full fitting and fixture as I never saw her with her gear off.

All I knew was she was a boy who looked like a girl with silicon tits who loved sucking dicks. Her name was Adele and she conned on to Mad Charlie at the Chevron nightclub.

We tried to tell Charlie that she was a transvestite but she already had a mouthful of him at the bar while a gang of us stood around blocking the view of onlookers and keeping guard.

I never claimed we were a toffy crew.

Within a month every pimp, hoon and parlour boss that this boy-girl had fallen out with over the previous twelve months in Melbourne had been hit by Mad Charlie's crew.

Then one night Mad Charlie fronts up, almost in tears.

'Adele is a bloke,' he said.

I mean how many times do you need to screw someone before you work out what sex they are. Was it the six o'clock shadow perhaps? The same thing happened when we hit the Crest Massage Parlour. Mad Charlie pumped the pants off a chick named Lee T who turned out to be a full sex-change transsexual in the 1970s.

Melbourne nightclubs and parlours were full of drag queens and transvestites. We knew most of 'em and they were all solid as rocks in a police station and good people but you could always spot them.

They were just too over the top, too much swing in the hips, too much tit showing, too show girlie.

They were like cartoons come to life, caricatures of real women. The voice was a giveaway and the look in the eye. To have sex with one and claim later you didn't know till after – well, OK, I'll let that go. Maybe you and your dick are mentally retarded. But for it to happen twice – I'm sorry. Really, you'd have to be blind, or going down a mineshaft, not to notice.

The fact is, Mad Charlie was a secret 'poo jammer'. It was one of the reasons Dave the Jew always held Charlie in disdain. You see, Mad Charlie was still allowing himself to be tricked by transvestites and transsexuals in the 1980s. Alphonse Gangitano was more open about his love of female impersonators, drag queens, transvestites and transsexuals.

I'm not condemning either man for being bisexual, only for being false pretenders.

The shooting of a parlour boss named Kelly in 1974 was the highlight of the year and as far as Mad Charlie and I were concerned Kelly's shooting proved to us that anything was possible.

Two young kids opened their eyes after that and saw that, as long as you were willing to back it up with blood, anything was possible.

Now to any police type person or prosecution lawyer who has shoplifted this book and read this, do not take what I have just said as a confession to any unsolved crime. It was just a small turning point I've made mention of, an example of how things can happen for a young couple who are prepared to work hard, etc., etc.

It didn't matter, anyway. Both Mad Charlie and myself were on our way by then with the help of Peter Rand. We could have controlled a large slice of Melbourne's prostitution industry by 1975 only Charlie and his dick got us pinched on a rape charge.

I was acquitted, Charlie was found guilty. Had that event not happened both Charlie and myself would have become entrenched in the world of so-called organised crime that year. Instead, Mad Charlie had to wait five years and I just launched myself into the world of the criminal mental case and totally disorganised crime.

It seemed a much better place to be at the time, although the superannuation wasn't so hot.

Organised criminals are generally killed by disorganised criminals. It sounds funny, but it happens to be true. The truth is that crime is only ever organised in the movies.

THERE is one good thing about being a so-called bestselling author. All sorts of people try to elbow their way between the pages of my next book. All I have to do is sit at the bar with a camera and they fall out of the woodwork. And I don't just mean sword swallowers and jelly-arsed whores.

All sorts.

As a married man I'm unable to take advantage of the various situations that present themselves. Indeed, I'm barely able to understand them, but my friends sometimes explain what's going on. Even if I did do anything naughty I couldn't write about it, but I swear I don't. It's the same with guns. I can no longer write about guns as by law I'm not allowed to have a gun and these days I obey the law.

It's all a bit hard when the subject matter of my books is made up of guns and girls, bullets and boobs. My wife tells me my books dwell too much on the sleazy and sordid and the police seem to be of the opinion that if I write about crime I must still be involved. Sometimes writing a book can be so difficult. I like to include photos but I then have to explain that a photo is just a photo. It means nothing, proves nothing. A photo is just salad dressing to add to the story. A little Asian chick sits down beside me and says, 'Whose camera is that?'

'Mine,' I reply.

'You not gonna use any photos of me in your book, are you?'

'No,' I say.

'Well, you can if you want. Nah, you better not. Nah, I don't care,' she continues.

All this was going on before I'd even taken a photo. Her name was Nickie Nguyen Vu Oanh. She spelt it out for me as I wrote it down. Now, mind you, all this is for a young lady who can't make her mind up about being in my book. I hadn't asked her if she would like to be and I hadn't requested a photo.

I sink a few more beers.

Nickie is wearing a bikini top and a pair of short shorts and a pair of knee-high boots under her dress. I know, because she whizzed the dress off when I handed the barmaid my camera.

'What will you say about me in your book, something nice?'

'Yes,' I replied.

'But you don't know me,' she went on. 'What will you say?'

I shook my head. 'I don't know. I'll think of something,' I said.

'You could take me to dinner,' said Nickie.

'My wife wouldn't like that,' I replied, 'but don't worry, I'll say something nice.'

Nickie smiled.

I took a few photos of her and I got the barmaid to snap off a few. Nickie was happy.

'I still haven't decided if I want to be in your book,' she said as I walked out of the bar.

'You've had your photo taken with me and given me the correct spelling of your name. Make up your mind,' I snapped.

'Yeah, OK.' She wiggled about on her stool like she had worms. 'But what will you say? If you took me to dinner you'd have something to write about,' she giggled.

I needed to take this chick to dinner like I needed another hole in the head. I looked at her and laughed and said something about writing about the silly things little girls say and do for a photo and a sentence or two in a book.

This final remark sort of went over Nickie's head but she sensed what I had just said could have been a very gently worded insult. It wasn't really an insult.

I've had females from all walks of life slide up to me in bars and proceed to chew my ears off (so to speak) with the story of their lives. 'You should write a fucking book,' I reply.

But that's too hard, of course. Why write a book when you can vomit your life story out to some poor no-eared bastard who is already writing one.

But among this river of cut glass I find a gem or two, stories well worth the telling, told to me by tits and legs that look like they stepped out of a magazine and me without my camera. But again I come back to being able to write about sex and crime without upsetting the people near to me and without meaning to do so.

I do seem to upset my wife. To check up on a story I may have to contact people, I may have to ring people up or write to people. Some of these people might be active criminals or ladies I know who came from a certain world. None of this sits well with a wife concerned that I not contact people from my past. Understandable and I agree smart but the books pay the bills and the books are crime stories.

It seems that to do anything in this life, at least in my life, I cannot do it without hurting the feelings of others. It's like people who go out of their way to push themselves between the pages of my books and there have been a few.

Nickie was one of the more harmless ones. They may get their wish and squeeze their way in but that don't mean they are going to like it when they get there. Who was it who said that people who write about people end up with no friends at all? Everyone wants to read about themselves but not everyone will like what they read.

MY mate Shane Farmer can spin yarns all night long and, like all great bar-room storytellers, for him the truth of the yarn isn't as important as the spinning of the story. The bar-room yarn is a fishing story: no one can say the bloke didn't go fishing ... it's just the size of the fish that he nearly caught that we smile at.

'You know when I took Alison to Las Vegas I gave her $300 to get her hair done,' said Shane. 'Now you'd think $300 would cover the fucking lady's hairdresser. When she came back her hair looked great.

'Give us some dough,' she asked.

'What? I gave you $300 before. Don't tell me a bloody hair-do cost $300.'

'Yeah, it did', replied Alison.

That $300 hair-do story is told and retold.

Shane knew Mad Charlie back in Charlie's walking-stick days. Charlie once fell off a ladder painting a house and did his ankle in and used a walking stick and took to hitting bouncers and nightclub staff with his stick when he went out at night.

Shane was forced to duck many a wild swing from Charlie's walking stick. His American yarns are the best. Let's face it. No one can call him a liar, because they weren't there.

If you tell a story about playing poker with Tony Bennett and Wayne Newton and the chief of detectives for the Las Vegas police, who's going to call you a liar?

If the guy tells me he met Sammy Davis Junior and Dean Martin in the late 1970s in Las Vegas and was once tossed down the stairs by three of Elvis Presley's bodyguards in a whore house in Memphis, Tennessee, who am I to question it?

Mad Charlie came back from America with a story that he had met and said hello to Don Carlo Gambino ... just the boss of all bosses of the American Mafia, that's all.

Alphonse Gangitano also came back from Italy with a truck load of stories about meeting with this or that Mafia boss but, personally, if I'm going to sit and listen to a fishing story I want to listen to one I can laugh at.

I mean what's the use of going overseas unless you can come back with some wild yarn? Ray Chuck always claimed he belted Reggie Kray in a prison in England. The opposite was the truth, maybe, but at least he did get to meet Reggie at the end of the fist.

Shane Farmer was in Las Vegas the day Howard Hughes died. The whole town stopped for a sixty-second silence.

Stories like that I can listen to, $300 hair cuts and poker games with singers I can listen to, Alison telling me about Miss Erotica contests and this Penthouse Pet blow-up doll telling the other girls in the dressing rooms that they may as well not bother because she had screwed all six judges.

She said she'd met all six judges beside the swimming pool that morning. The only problem was, laughed Alison, the real judges were women involved in the magazine, modelling and beauty industry.

Miss Smartarse had screwed six blokes all right. Only problem for her was that they had all been judges in the two previous contests.

Let us now turn to some other myths, legends and folk stories. First, the myth.

GET the big bastard pissed. I want him mellow and easy to handle was the word. OK, it's 16 March 1998, and Chopper Read turned up pissed on the set for the first episode of Libby Gorr's new live-to-air ABC TV series *McFeast*.

Of course Elle and the whole TV crew claimed not to have known how much I had drunk. Bullshit. I had drunkenly annoyed half the female staff in the place. I even draped a drunken arm around Tina Arena as I sucked on a can of beer and joked with her about the death of Alphonse. Tina is a little Sicilian girl from the western suburbs of Melbourne. She's met more gangsters than I have.

Tina was concerned for my state and alerted the ABC staff that Chopper looked a bit pissed to her. Don't tell me that no one told Elle that there was a pissed-out-off-his-head, no-eared bloke backstage. Elle gambled that a drunken Chopper Read would be more fun than a sober one.

Elle didn't want to put her little Jewish girl university undergraduate sense of humour up against mine unless I was drunk to the point of not being able to speak. It was the same in the crime world. I always dealt with people who had more to lose than me.

Having said that, it was my own fault. I didn't have to drink as much as I did and I could have just continued to lay on the floor of the Green Room and refused to walk on stage. It wasn't Elle's fault.

Most guests are given a few quiet wines to mellow them out before they go on.

I'm sure that is all Elle wanted. I don't think she believed that I was as drunk as she was told I was. The point was that Elle was told. Tina Arena was concerned enough about me to speak up and say something a good hour before I went on, but that's showbusiness. I went on and made an idiot of myself and Elle and the ABC allowed me to do so, claiming they had no idea that I was drunk till I walked out on to the set. Libby then realised I was so pissed I could hardly speak.

Mellow is one thing, but her staff had allowed me to get into a near coma. Not that it would be that easy to stop me. After the show Elle ran up to me in the street outside the studio as I was leaving and with her dressing gown flapping in the breeze threw herself into my drunken arms.

'Thanks, Chopper.'

'I'm a bit pissed, Elle. I'm sorry,' I slurred.

She laughed. 'I was thinking of going into another line of work anyway. Ha, ha.'

She knew I'd just fucked up her television career, but she thanked me for coming on her show and ordered two security blokes to drive me to my hotel. Libby had overplayed her hand. I had nothing to lose. She had everything. She gambled and she lost but she did it with charm, dignity, a smile, good humour and grace.

But, Elle, don't you ever tell anyone that you didn't know that I was just a little bit tipsy before the show.

You'll come back, baby, and I hope your live TV days are more promising than mine are. Ha, ha.

Postscript: when I got back to my hotel I began some serious drinking.

LET'S kill all the lawyers. A wealthy man called his three best friends to his death bed. They were a doctor, a politician and a lawyer. He told each man he wanted to take his money with him when he died. He then gave each man a million dollars and made each man swear to toss the money into his grave after the funeral.

Afterwards, the doctor asked the politician, 'Did you toss in all the money?

'Well, not quite,' replied the politician. 'I needed half a million for my re-election campaign and a further two hundred thousand for home renovations and another two hundred thousand for the new medical wing that is being named after me but I did toss in a hundred thousand. I'm sure the good Lord and the dear departed will understand.'

'Yes,' said the doctor. 'Speaking of medical wings, I donated half a million to the medical research unit being named after me and I'm afraid I bought a new car and a new house.'

'So how much did you toss into the grave?' asked the politician. The doctor, looking embarrassed, said, 'seventy-five thousand.'

The lawyer, listening in silence, shook his head in disgust.

'Gentlemen, I'm ashamed of the both of you. I simply cannot believe what I'm hearing,' said the lawyer.

The doctor and politician both looked at the lawyer and spoke at once.

'How much did you toss in, then?' they asked.

The lawyer held his head up and with a note of pride in his voice said, 'Needless to say, gentlemen, I tossed in a cheque for the full amount.' It's an old joke but it holds true today. When a lawyer does you a favour look close, count all your fingers after shaking his hand and kiss your money goodbye. Oh, and don't forget to thank him afterwards. I've sat in a lot of court rooms and I've had meetings with a lot of lawyers and I still haven't met one lawyer who hasn't tried to talk to me like I'm a mental retard. Criminal lawyers spend most of their time talking to criminals and most criminals are mental retards, therefore the lawyer does develop a superiority complex. It's an occupational hazard, I suppose.

Lawyers in civil and family law spend most of their time with clients who haven't got a legal clue. Again, this only feeds the ego of the monster – the lawyer, that is. And then we come to the Queen's Counsel, and what a yellow brick road we then proceed to skip up. Ha, ha.

Female lawyers can have a great bedside manner but are prone to losing cases. Never allow the charms of a lady lawyer to sway you from common sense. I'd love to tell some stories but the thought of being sued prevents me, not to mention my publishers. Let's just say I knew of one lady lawyer who wore stockings and a suspender belt, stiletto high heels and the works under her black dress and robe and would allow a certain client to run his hand up her leg in the Supreme Court interview room. She would be explaining why the case was hopeless and the client was telling her not to worry about it as he pumped half his hand into her.

When a guy is locked up in prison the mind can play tricks.

When a lady lawyer pops into the prison on a Sunday wearing

runners and a baggy tracksuit and the poor prisoner is called up to the professional visit area to see his lawyer and the tracksuit pants come down and she invites the client to hump the arse off her it tends to soften the word guilty.

Of course when all is legally lost and the inmate hears tall tales about some bloke in the remand yard getting a blow job from his lady lawyer whenever she visits him, common sense finally hits home and it's 'you're sacked' time and 'has anyone got the phone number of a good QC?'

Let's face it, knob polishers don't win court cases. Of course, none of this ever happened to me and I've never met such a woman but I have heard some wild yarns, believe it or not. But if your lawyer shows close and personal how she can suck the chrome off a tow ball and you're paying her from your own funds it's hard to accuse her of robbing you – by such tricks as wiping the whole firm's phone account off on to your bill and having large slabs of money held in trust spent on mindless nonsense – when you're about to shoot your bolt.

No bloke wants to argue about money, but as I said none of this ever happened to me, perish the thought.

There was one high-flying lawyer who wanted me to do a certain media interview. I then find out that the female reporter in question has the lawyer on a promise. If Chopper does the interview the lawyer gets to play sink the sausage with said reporter.

Needless to say I didn't do the interview and I fell out with the lawyer. After all, this lady reporter was all tits and legs, so why should some lawyer get all the goodies? He was getting her and I'd earn his undying gratitude. This isn't some legal aid hack, mind you. This prick earns top dollar and he still wants me to get him laid. Legally, it made no sense at all to me.

There was a faggot lawyer in Melbourne who got caught in an extremely compromising position with a client in Pentridge, which proves there is something for everyone in this field. I know lawyers love a brief but this is ridiculous.

There was one lady lawyer in Melbourne who openly told clients that she worked her way through uni doing escort work Friday and Saturday nights for a good four years solid – and she still put in the odd night or two once a month, having bought her own escort agency. She would visit Pentridge regularly and I'd bump into her now and again, so to speak. I'd never hired her legally – or professionally, for that matter – but I knew her history. I mean, this was an open secret. She socialised with criminals and lawyers after hours and from all accounts was a nice lady to know. There was another girl working in a strip club in Melbourne after she finished her law degree. A couple of pissed partners of a major law firm were examining her while she did the splits on a table and ended up giving her a job in the firm. What is Latin for 'show us your tits', I wonder?

But again I return to the QC. Mental illness or alcoholism must come with the territory.

One QC I knew who later became a Supreme Court justice spent several hours in the Supreme Court cells telling me about him seeing a UFO while travelling across the Nullabor Plain. That was fine, compared with the rest of the conversation ... when he told me he was a member of an organisation that believed Jesus Christ, Mohammad, Buddha and Adolf Hitler were, in fact, visitors from outer space sent to correct human history. This bloke was dead-set insane, certifiable.

We have had pedophile judges. In fact shirt-lifters and pedophiles in the judiciary are commonplace. The more prominent of these have taken their own lives.

I've seen one QC who would ask for an adjournment so he could polish off a quarter-bottle of vodka in the toilet. Then he'd come back and win the case.

All I can say about lawyers is that criminals are the only people desperate enough and dumb enough to hire the turds.

MICHELE Bennett, the producer of the *Chopper* movie, rang to say it's a goer. I suspect that she is quite mad but I admire her dash. She has been knocked back and knocked back, she's had doors shut in her face and she's kept going. We all said sorry for previous cross words and kissed and made up as people in the arts do.

Art is a three-letter word for bullshit in my opinion but the movie has finally begun. It only took them nearly seven years.

I should be plonked up the bottom with a large rubber gumboot for doubting the buggers in the first place. Shame on me. Speaking of Shane, I got mad drunk again the other night at the Richmond Arms Hotel.

Evidently, so I'm told, I picked Stacy the barmaid up and gave her a shoulder ride around the bar. Maybe I'm part elephant. I'll leave you to imagine which part.

I don't recall any of this, mind you. Mary-Ann had to come and collect me yet again. Maybe I should get her an ambulance. She was not pleased. If I don't tone my drunken conduct down divorce is in the air. Mary-Ann will stand for no more and I will have to go and live above a pub.

That didn't sound too bad but then again I don't want to lose my wife, home, child, cats, chickens, dog and all I've worked for just because of the demon drink, so I must sober myself and conduct myself in a manner befitting a bestselling author and landed gentry chicken farmer.

At long last I've encountered a person I'm quite fearful of ... my wife. And there'll be no ha ha about that. It's no laughing matter.

ALISON Downes and Shane Farmer came around the other day. They have turned out to be quite good friends. Miss Nude Australia and my wife get along quite well, which proves that it is an odd world we live in. Whenever I walk into the Richmond Arms with Alison you can hear a pin, or a prick, drop. I mean the lady is built like a blow-up doll and Shane has a voice louder than mine.

'Hey, Chopper, you drinking?' he yells at the top of his lungs. What a stupid question. Would you yell, 'Hey, Linda, you swallowing?' or 'Hey, fish, you swimming?'

He then proceeds to tell people with great comedy what an arsehole I am. Complaining that whenever I come to his nightclub I cause trouble and play up.

I drink my beer in silence then mutter, 'Shut up, Shane. You're red lighting me you air-raiding bastard.'

But I deserve to be the butt of comic jest at the hands of mates and anger at the hands of my wife. My conduct after partaking of drink is getting quite out of hand. The trouble is that when you've been inside for so long there is a natural desire to catch up for lost time. When you know you should go home, you still fear you may miss out on some adventure. It's just not in my nature to say, 'No thanks, I must go home because there's a good documentary on penguin mating on the ABC and the video's broken.'

SADNESS and much tears befell our happy household a while ago. Mary-Ann was heartbroken. Our two dogs, Ronnie and Reggie, had to be shot, or put to sleep as they say. They were named after the Pommy gangsters, the Kray brothers, only they were marginally more dangerous.

Ronnie (aka Master Splinter) had previously killed sheep with Reggie egging him on, or was that Reggie with Ronnie egging him on? They worked as a team. Fox terrier, Jack Russell cross breeds, with a touch, I think, of wolverine.

They both went in for the kill but to Mary-Ann they were her most loyal and faithful little friends and she doted on them. I covered for them the last time they killed a sheep. On a property there is no court of appeal for a farm dog with a taste for warm mutton, but when they killed a sheep I would go into a cover-up mode quicker than Richard Nixon. I suppose my experience in getting rid of corpses and cleaning up bloodstains in a former life came in handy when trying to save the dogs from themselves.

Mary-Ann remained staunch to the dogs even when she knew they were killers. But then again, she's married me so I suppose it shouldn't have come as a surprise.

But the beginning of the end came when Mary-Ann bought me a giant pure-bred Sussex Fowl, a hen with thirteen chicks. We named her Gloria Swanson. She was the biggest, most magnificent chicken you ever saw. A giant of a bird that looked more like an emu than a chicken and within moments of her arrival Gloria Swanson took over the barn yard. She was a proud mother and her thirteen little yellow chicks followed her about all over the place. Any attempt to get near would have Gloria Swanson flying at you in a wild rage. She was not to be taken lightly.

Even the African guinea fowls, who are no chickens, ran when the great Gloria Swanson came near. Big deal, you poultry illiterates cry. Well, let me tell you the guinea fowls can slice human flesh with their beaks and are indeed a vicious, ill-tempered bird but no match for this mother Sussex hen.

Then came the day. I was having my afternoon nap, as creative writing and a bottle of bourbon can take it out of you, when I was woken up by Mary-Ann's screams.

I ran outside to see Ronnie fighting with Gloria Swanson. Rotten Ronnie had dug his way out of his pen. Ronnie had torn the arse out of Gloria Swanson but the big hen fought on, feet and feathers flying in a desperate effort to protect her chicks.

I broke the fight up and put Ronnie back in his pen, then I picked up the savagely wounded Gloria Swanson. She was torn nearly in half but alive. I put her back in her pen and she called her chicks to her.

All thirteen came out of hiding and ran to their dying mother. Gloria Swanson seemed to be counting her chicks and all of them gathered around then the big hen died. Mary-Ann was in tears and so was I.

Isn't that weird? I have seen men die, seen bodies, poured lime on the cold corpses of drug dealers who deserved to die and then stopped for a mixed grill on the way home, yum.

But the sight of Big Gloria dying while she fought for her chicks was too much for old Chop.

The dogs had to go. Paul Manning came up and shot them for us. Ronnie for killing and Reggie because he would only fret to death without his brother. I buried them both under a pine tree and the tears in the house lasted a full week.

All the Sussex chicks survived and now are giant great hens and roosters. All of them led by a giant hen we have named Gloria Simpson, daughter of the late Gloria Swanson. If she had been skinny we would have called her Gloria Marshall.

It is a little spooky because we can still hear Ronnie and Reggie around the property. No, the claw hammer I got in the skull all those years back is not finally kicking in ... it is our pet magpie, Eddie, who imitates the sound of the dogs howling. Little Eddie's cage hung above their pen and the magpie had grown up to mimic the sound of the dogs. Then one day Eddie died and there was no more barking.

Until, that is, Ronnie and Reggie were replaced with a Jack Russell puppy named Little Bill and Little Eddie was replaced with a cocky named Paul. As the farmers say, when you have livestock you have dead stock. That's life, I guess.

CHAPTER 8

TASSIE CHAINSAW MASSACRE

'Only a drunk or a madman would survive – luckily, on that occasion, I was both.'

WHEN I got out of jail I thought my days of conflict and angst were behind me but, as usual, I was wrong.

I was to be the catalyst of the greatest amount of local upset on the old farm for years. Every freeloader and scavenger for miles around has been playing on my father-in-law's Christian goodwill and kind nature, and cutting themselves tons of wood each winter – all free, gratis and for nothing. So, as you would, I bought the timber lease, chained the gate and put up a timber lease notice and Keep Out signs.

Instead of getting the hint that the days of free wood were over they expected my father-in-law and me to get the wood for them.

For Christ's sake, we are running a farm not a public charity. People who expect others to look after 'em free of charge are called bludgers or politicians in Australia. The only trouble is that Aussie land is now so full of bludgers the bastards now outnumber us law-abiding, hard-working folk.

READY'S RUN

'Twas just a hundred acres, or maybe two or three
Old Hodge's' Hill seemed to run for as far as the eye could see
And for years the locals came and cut their loads of winter wood
Ten ton a year for every man; my God, them times was good

Then came along a city bloke with a bit of dash and cash
And thought that all this wood for free was being rather rash
These freeloaders and bludgers have had their load of fun
I'll buy the lot and chain the gate and call it Ready's Run
And now up on the Hill the chainsaw sings its song.
No more for you, you bludging scum,
you had it free far too long

And as the trees come falling down old Ready's getting richer
And the local boys are spitting chips
'cause they couldn't see the picture.
But what no-one understood and what few still understand
Was that they treated it like it was theirs,
though they never owned the land
So now one man cuts the firewood and he cuts it just for fun
While all the rest freeze to death cursing Ready's Run.
Ha ha.

– Mark Brandon Read

AS A city boy with simple tastes, I find the bush great fun. I've always been an adaptable fellow and I've quite taken to country life. Chainsawing the guts out of everything is great fun. It's nowhere near as good as turning up the heat on a drug dealer, but it's still better than nude Twister.

Trees are in their own way far more dangerous than drug dealers. Put the chainsaw to a drug dealer and they will wriggle and scream and beg and moan. They'll call to God and call their mates on the mobile phone and everything's sweet. But when you give it to a tree at night it can pay you back big time.

One time under moonlight I was giving a big gum the big slash when it paid me back. I have always believed that all things are based on logic. To me it seems perfectly logical to cut a tree down with a chainsaw at night by the light of the moon without being sure which way they may fall. It's sort of Russian Roulette with a giant hardwood.

I reckon some trees have their own personalities. Some give up once the chainsaw cuts into them, but others have knots in them that buck the cutter all the way through. And then when you are through the bastards, they still turn on you in death. They should fall one way but they can come back on you.

If you're cutting it on a slope, then CRASH, the bloody thing lands on your cool box and a dozen cans of cold beer are lost.

One missed me by a whisker. I was crashing through the bush as the tree started to come after me. They reckon you can outrun a tree – after all, it doesn't even have runners, but they keep coming very fast. And in the dark it's luck, either good or bad, on which way it falls. As I ran in the dark I knew that if I lived I would always remember the following three lessons …

Lesson one: never cut a tree down at night;

Lesson two: never cut a tree down at night when you are pissed;

Lesson three: if you do cut a tree down at night when you are pissed, make sure the cool box is in a protected spot.

I was about to say if you haven't done this you haven't lived – and if you do it too many times you bloody well won't live long either.

Imagine it, having avoided being killed by Nazis, Mafia nitwits, Romanian crazies, psychotic coppers and sick puppies of all descriptions, the old Chopper could have cashed in his (wood) chips, care of a hundred-year-old blue gum.

THE two hundred ton of timber on my hundred acre wood lease could be three to four hundred ton but I will need a tractor and a heap of chainsaw work to pull it out.

Why is honest work so hard?

In the old days you'd just wave a chainsaw near a drug dealer and he'd put a grand in your hand just out of good manners. Now as a man of the land I am expected to work like a slave around sheep shit and flies just to keep the wolf from the door.

It also seems I've got the only wood lease around these parts. Farmers don't sell them anymore. Naturally, the 'Chopper the wood merchant jokes' are flying thick and fast. I've had some close calls. Chainsaw in hand on a hill on a really windy day, pissed as a parrot, I cut down through a sixty foot dead tree at a forty five degree angle without cutting a scarfe into the tree on the other side.

I heard a crack and pulled the chainsaw out then ran, the wind twisted the tree and I heard another crack, and as I ran the tree followed me. I was about forty feet away through the scrub as the tree fell all over me, smashing me to the ground.

I still had my chainsaw going and laying on my guts I cut my way out. Only a drunk or a madman would survive – luckily, on that occasion, I was both. I've decided never again to go near the bush pissed with a chainsaw. The old bushies reckon I cut them down on guts and sheer good luck and they marvel at how I'm still alive.

I approach a tree with an attitude of 'you'll drop or I will, you bastard'. It's total insanity – but I love it, ha, ha.

I HAVE met and dealt with some two-faced treacherous maggots in my time and the bloke from the bush would hold his own in any company. If it's not nailed down, it will get pinched; if it's borrowed it will never be returned, and gossip and slander are the only topics of conversation.

Most of the country people I've met could get work as trick knife tossers in any circus because sticking knives in people's backs is their favourite pastime. I could give you example after example.

Kindness is always treated as weakness and a laugh at the expense of another is the only laugh to be had. Is it any wonder that Paterson was embraced by a nation while old Henry Lawson stood in his shadow. Paterson gave a nation a romantic myth and, given the choice between a myth and the truth, people will always take the myth. I won't be thanked for pointing this out – then again, neither was Lawson. At least he had his own ears.

I've always maintained that there are exceptions and contradictions to every rule of law. I've noted that bushmen of the old school, farmers, men of the land, the landed gentry of the generation that lived through the Great Depression, World War Two, bush fires and floods and droughts are a different class to your modern day country folk.

Lawson was born in a tent and spent his life in and out of Darlinghurst jail and viewed life through a bottle. I won't hang my hat on every word he said but will say that I have met some true blue gentlemen, some real old-time salt of the earth country folk whose word is their bond and whose handshake can be taken to the grave.

I hold my own father-in-law up as such a man – old E.V. Hodge. But, alas, men of his calibre are a fast-dying breed. He probably won't thank me for mentioning his name but I'd like to say that he is among the few truly good men I've met. You wouldn't meet a better man than Ernest Vincent in a day's march and I thank him for his kindness to me.

I'm attempting to try to get my gun licence back. Well, that's not strictly accurate as I've not ever had one. Like Rolf Harris, I'm a big-picture man and can't get caught up on little details. I've written to the Commissioner of Police for Tasmania, John Johnston, requesting that the section 130 of the Firearms Act 1996 prohibiting me from possessing or using a firearm be lifted. Assistant Commissioner of Police Barry Bennett often drinks at my local pub, the Richmond Arms Hotel, and he reckons I've got no chance at all. However, I will continue to put my case forward.

After all, I'm a farmer now, a middle-aged man, the fat bloke in the white T-shirt. Who ever heard of a farmer without a shotgun? Has the whole world gone mad? Am I to wrestle tiger snakes and wild dogs?

ANYWAY, back to business. In the immortal words of Peter Sellers I will now whistle the soliloquy from *Hamlet.* I often dream of Mad Charlie and Alphonse, and in my dreams they are alive and well, although badly wounded, and we sit at the bar drinking.

I awake from these dreams deeply disturbed. Just when I think that the past is the past except for my writing about it, I find myself drinking with them in my dreams.

It shows me that none of us can ever leave the past. It lies dormant in the back of our skulls and like a dirty big wombat, comes out at night for a sniff around and a scratch.

The wogs have spent the best part of the 1990s getting themselves murdered. Gentle Joe Quadara, Steve the Greek Caracasidis, Alphonso 'Fat Al' Muratore, Alphonse Gangitano, Vincenzo Mannella, his brother Gerry, Danny Boy Mendoza, Mad Charlie Hegyalji, Antonio 'Little Tony' Peluso and several more over the last nine years who never made the papers or police attention – as they simply went on the missing list. About twelve all up, I can think of. However, their names escape me as I write this and would continue to escape me if I was called before any nosy coroners who wanted my opinions under oath.

To any judges who want to get a few ideas about where the truth might be – buy this book like everyone else.

I'll say this. A vanished body is strictly business. A body left to be found is a warning. My goodness, it is such a puzzle to try to work out what is going on. 'Mafia' is a handy word to toss up when the police and media don't have the faintest idea. If the body smells of garlic and lead then the cops and the hacks scream 'Mafia'.

It makes good headlines, and takes the pressure off the detectives because no one expects them to solve Mafia killings.

I've learnt from bitter experience never to give my opinion in writing or the spoken word without great caution on matters relating to unsolved police cases. Ten or twenty years down the track when it's all old history a crew of old reporters and police will gather for drinks and say, 'You know old "no ears" told us all way back then and we thought it was a joke. If you strip it back he told the truth in his own roundabout, half-mad, comic way years ago and none of us believed him.'

It's like Flannery. I told everyone the bum got put through a tree shredder. Since then quite a few top men in the police, media and criminal world have claimed to know the real truth and some have even stated they knew where the dog was buried.

So where's the body? Ha, ha. Tree mulch is still my tip.

Then again, what would I know? I'm just a roaring drunk, a hopeless liar or a roaring liar and a hopeless drunk, or so some would have you believe.

But I didn't get these scars in a fight over the sushi tray at a crime writers' conference, and the claw hammer hole in my head didn't come from a dispute with the scone lady over the strawberry jam.

No one believes a word I say, not while there are chaps about with a better yarn to spin. Hitmen in Australia aren't vast in number. It is quite a small fraternity and not an Olympic event. They may not march together on Anzac Day but they know each others' names.

Either we know each other personally or by reputation. If two hitmen don't know each other they would both know of or have a mutual friend.

They may live thousands of kilometres apart and be loners but there is an invisible thread around the nation that links them all together.

They all have friends within the illegal arms industry, as small-arms ordinance is vital to the professional killer's line of work and, naturally, every man and his dog knows Mark Brandon Read understands about small-arms ordinance.

Long before the coppers have a clue, a hitman will know who has done a killing. He will know the style and the type of murder – and will know whose trademark it is likely to be.

There are, so rumour goes, men who know so much about the illegal sale of small arms ordinance that they only have to find out the calibre and make of the weapon used to track down the individual who bought it within about three days.

Arms dealers sell weapons but only a limited amount of ammo and no extra clips for autos or general spare parts. All in all, both worlds are small and close knit. Why things are done is no one's business but who did what and for how much isn't hard to find out. Of course, this is just rumour. But as they say, where there is gunsmoke there is usually gunfire.

Myself, as a gentleman farmer, wood chopper and father of a young boy, I steer clear of these matters of blood and guts. These days I am more interested in Hans Christian Andersen than Christopher Dale Flannery. Ha, ha.

I can now leave all that to the heavy-thinking boys, the police and media. They have read all the books and watched all the movies so they would have to know, wouldn't they?

Some coppers live by the rule of the Mounties, 'We always get our man,' – or was that 'Let's club those baby seals'? I can't remember.

I wonder what wise advice I could give all these smart young crime solvers. Texas Bix Bender said it best.

'Don't squat with your spurs on, boys.'

The cops and robbers of today are a pack of junior 'G Spot' men in pursuit of a bunch of bubble-gum gangsters. As for the modern-day homicide squad investigating the so-called Mafia murders of the 1990s, in my opinion they put the Haw in Hee Haw.

Sometimes you can see best from the outside looking in, but in the world of the professional hitman this is not the case.

There is a one-way mirror. If you don't belong you look in the mirror, scratch your nuts, pull a couple of nose hairs out and be on your way. You have no idea what is on the other side.

Reporters and coppers exchange theories and earnest looks but most times they are just guessing, at best, or making it up, at worst.

They throw a line in the water and just hope. Sometimes they get a bite but it is based on dumb luck, not great knowledge. After all, they charged me with murdering Sammy the Turk just because I took half his head off with a shotgun.

Any fool could see that it was a clear-cut case of self-defence that resulted in him getting a terminal migraine. Luckily the jury had a better understanding than the lawyers and the coppers, and I was found not guilty, which was a triumph of our justice system.

I've just been told to stop all that writing nonsense and chop some wood for the fire. In Tassie you can have the greatest train of thought and be writing it down as you slowly die from the cold. Now, I have already suffered for my art so excuse me while I warm up.

First I chainsaw half a day in the bush and cart it home. Now I've got to chop it all up with a wood splitter. Well, I don't mind the thorns, because my wife is such a rose. Ha, ha.

Sawn-off shotguns, chainsaws, tiger snakes and wives. If you don't take a firm grip they can jump back and bite you.

I'm just a friendly, country fella.

Top: We have a lot in common … they shot a movie, I shot people.

Above: Film guru Andrew Dominik.

Me with my alter ego, Eric Bana, a top fella. But get your ears off mate.

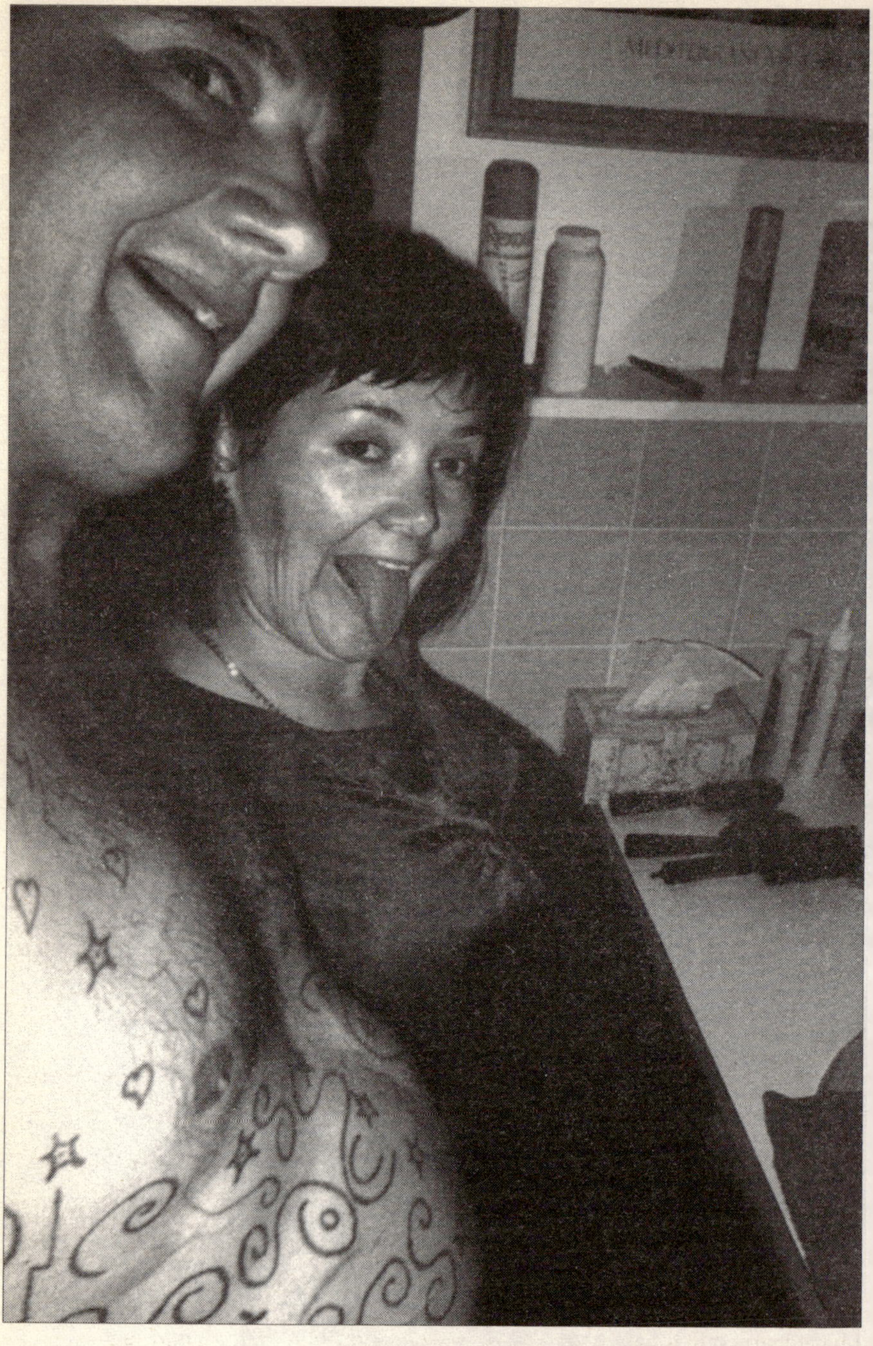

Mary-Ann was pregnant … I went out in sympathy.

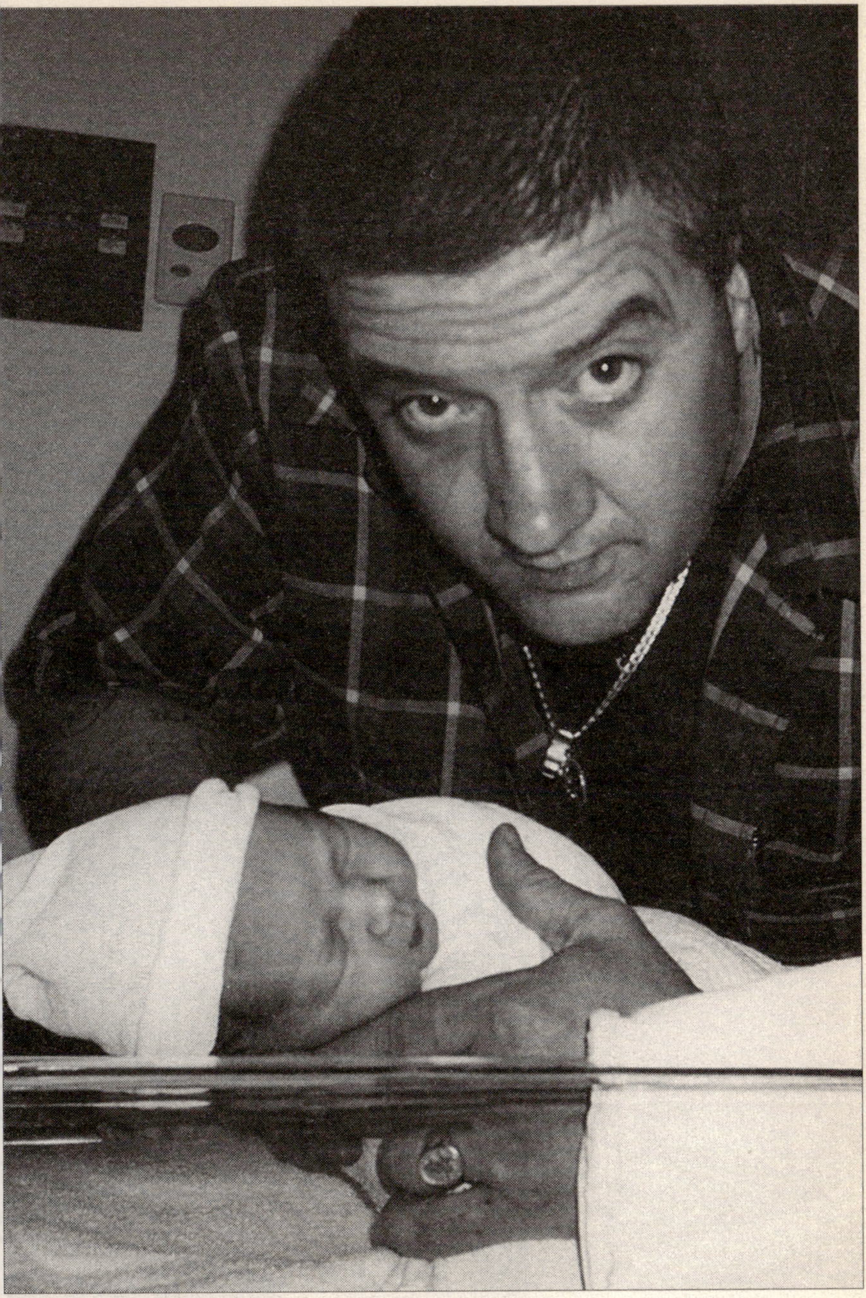

I have learned that babies are like drug dealers … they cry a lot and shit themselves.

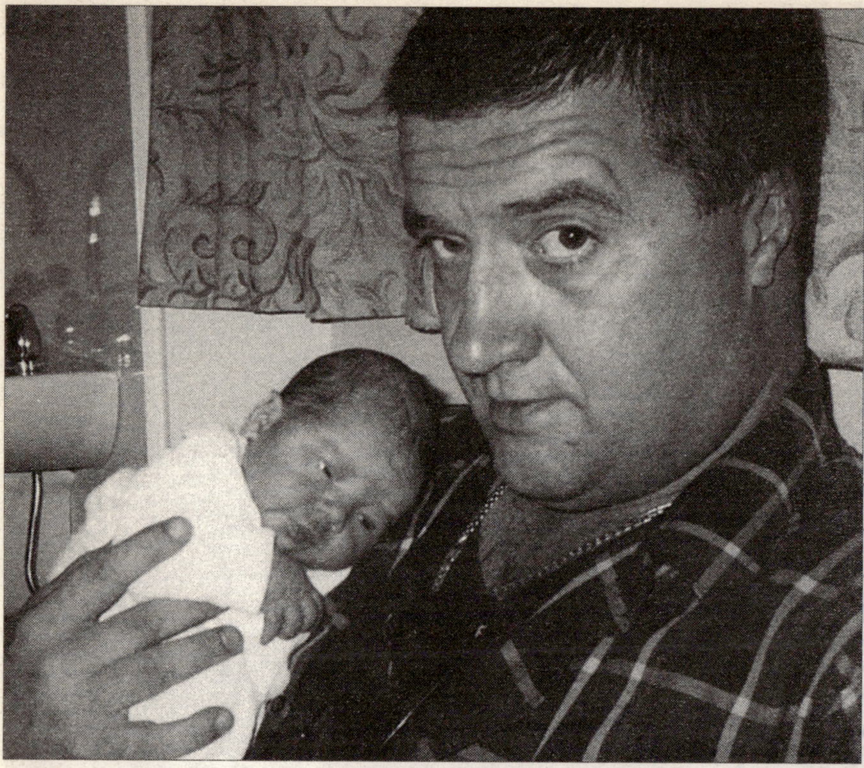

Me with Charles Vincent.
He has changed my life …
I have changed his nappies.

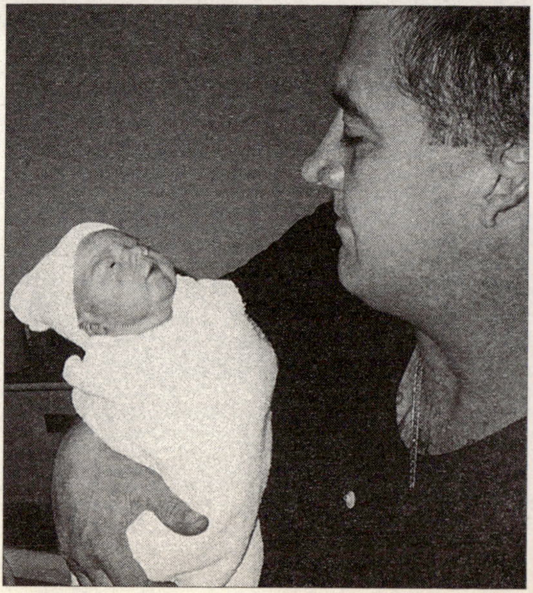

Kellie Russell … a top, honest journalist

CHAPTER 9

HAUNTING THE OLD HAUNTS

'Evidently there was a no-eared gentleman in the club who would not surrender his overcoat.'

MEANWHILE, back at the mental hospital, Mister Read was taking his morning medication as he got off the plane at Melbourne Airport. It was Saturday, 5 June 1999 – my first time in Melbourne as a free man in more than ten years.

When I was released in 1991 I left straight for Tassie, so I was looking forward to seeing the old town again. I knew I could be there for about twenty-four hours before nervous crims would come looking. They would assume that if I was in town I would be after them so, out of panic, they may do something stupid.

Neil Diamond was in concert at Melbourne and Mary-Ann wanted to see him so over we went. I'd arranged to see Colin Dix and his wife Simone. Colin is the producer of my two CDs *The Smell of Love* and *Get Your Ears Off* – both underrated classics that will surely become collectors' items.

After that I had to see my twin publishers, Sly and Greedy. I had arranged to see 'Loxy' – Robert Lochrie and his wife Jenny and several others – but I had to ring up and tell them I wasn't coming. I'm sorry about missing them, but you can fit only so much into an overnight visit to Melbourne and I didn't want to argue with friends over who to see and where to go with no real time to do any of it.

I don't like to leave the farm and Melbourne is now a strange land to me. All my old friends and enemies are dead – or at least look as if they ought to be. Most of them are gone and for me the heart of

Melbourne was in the heart of my friends and, yes, even my enemies and now that heart is missing for me. Melbourne is only a sentimental memory and seeing it again made me cry inside.

We stayed at Le Meridien at Rialto, Collins Street, Melbourne. American Express all the way. If I had a cat small enough I may have been able to swing it in the room they gave us.

Mary-Ann and I met up with Colin and Simone and we made our way to the restaurant. We ordered our meals and drinks. The service was slack, and after thirty minutes I got a steak that wouldn't fill Karen Carpenter.

The $127 bill for the meal was equally on the nose. All in all I reckon you'd get better accommodation, food, booze and service if you were in witness protection, which is saying something.

Snobbery and poshness is all very lah de dah and nice but over-priced booze and small meals along with slow service followed up with a 'you're not one of us, we don't want you here' attitude is not my idea of a good time.

Small hint for the novice traveller as well: always travel with your own toilet paper.

Anyway, it was good to see Colin and Simone. Colin is quite a normal-type person face to face and not at all the mental case I took him to be. Whereas Sly and Greedy both drink like there is no tomorrow and hold a conversation by the throat. We drank at the bar of Le Meridien from about 5.30pm until 11.30pm, then made our way to an Irish pub for some sort of Irish stew, stout and beef potato pie and glasses of Irish Whisky – my publishers are always very health conscious and always have all the food groups.

I made my way past the Irish as Paddy's pigs waiters, waitresses and general staff to the upstairs toilet and just happened to see inside the kitchen.

The cook in this Irish pub was a Chinaman, no doubt from that old Irish clan of Wong Fung O'Reilly.

Well, that was about it for me. Let's get out of here and back to Le Meridien for more drinkies – as you would.

We walked up a dark Melbourne lane and saw some dapper-looking little chap walk past, talking into his mobile phone. Then he called out and came back. He said he was in charge of a modelling agency and wanted to take some photos of me. Now, I might have tickets on myself but I never thought of me as a Calvin Klein type. It was only when I had a look at Sly and Greedy that I realised that I was the good-looking one.

I asked him if he'd run out of models with no ears and he let out a nervous giggle and wandered off. And they call me crazy.

As a wise man once wrote, the night quietly sank into a bottle of beer as I waved Sly and Greedy goodbye.

I saw Sly look at me with a hint of concern. Was I returning to the Le Meridien or heading off into the night? Do leopards change their spots? How would I know, do I look like David Attenborough?

I knew of a club run by a Chinese lady not too far away, just off King Street. And there were various clubs in Chinatown, a few brothels run by friends of mine from the 1970s and dance clubs still controlled by Chopper Read friendly people so I just walked blindly about in the night, viewing a lost city, almost wishing Alphonse was still alive.

I got up to Lygon Street and just stood and looked at a street alive with Generation X nothing people. No one recognised me except for one old man.

As I turned to walk back toward the city I heard a 'Hey, Chopper'. This old guy had run a restaurant in Lygon Street since the late 1960s. He must have been in his seventies … whereas I just felt as if I was. I won't mention his name or his business as it would not be healthy for him. We stood and talked.

'Chopper, you back? Good to see you. You want coffee, something to eat? Come in, come in.'

'No, Poppa,' I replied, 'I'm sweet, I just come for a look see.'

'A look see for what?' said Poppa. 'I'm selling up. Fuck it, I'm too old for this shit. All the good boys, they all gone. Now yuppies and Italian yuppies, they look at you with the eyes and smile but they got no heart, no guts, no dash, no style, they no can explain,' said Poppa.

'Greedy, self-centred little turds,' I replied.

'Yeah,' said Poppa. 'Fucking selfish turds.'

'Spoilt,' I said.

'Yeah,' replied old Poppa, 'spoilt.'

As I walked away the old man called to me, 'Hey, Chopper, I loved Alphonse like my own son, but I love you too.'

I waved and walked on. That was always the problem with big Al and me. A lot of his friends were my friends as well. It almost makes me want to cry. But not quite.

I WALKED down King Street. Two girls came smashing down a flight of stairs, all fists, feet and teeth. One chick was kicking the living guts out of the other. They both fell at my feet.

'Hi you, Chopper.' A big pair of eyes and a wide smile beamed up at me.

'How you going?' I replied.

One lady got to her feet and kicked the other in the head. It was a full-stop to their animated interaction.

'Piss off, you moll,' she hissed as the bloodied and beaten loser scurried away.

The winner straightened herself up. Really big eyes, really big smile, lips and teeth, big boobs, long legs, micro mini-skirt and high heels. Stockings, suspenders.

It wasn't *TV Ringside* gear but I wasn't complaining. She was a dancer off duty and fighting drunk.

'Hey, Chopper, my boyfriend would love your fucking autograph.' She had a way with words.

She had more chance of getting it than he did and she looked like a girl who was used to getting her own way. She had a smile that would suck the lead out of a shotgun shell. This chick was a weapon.

Drunk, fun loving and almost wearing hardly any clothes at all, she wasn't *The Flying Nun*. She was the sort of girl you'd take home to meet Mum providing your mum needed a good smack in the mouth or a broken bottle in the neck.

Her name was Monique, or at least that's what she told me. My name was Chopper, or at least that's what I told her, while staring at her ample chest, which appeared to be staring back.

A big-eyed, big mouth, big tits, long legs, wiggle when she walks, giggle when she talks Polish chick whose dad was or used to be a prison officer in Pentridge with me when I was an inmate. I won't mention his last name for fear of embarrassment at Pentridge staff reunions.

I thought how stupid I was not to realise immediately that with a name like Monique she would be Polish, wouldn't she?

This chick could talk the leg off an elephant and probably deep throat one as well, from the look of her. She had a mouth wider than Mick Jagger's. As a married man I am no longer meant to notice these things, but as an author I am allowed to. It's called literary licence, and it's a lot easier to get than a gun licence. So you can all get stuffed.

She walked along with me in the night, chattering away. Most Pentridge prison officers back when I was there told their kids Chopper Read bedtime stories. Her Polish father told young Monique quite a few. As we walked along I couldn't help thinking that I would have liked to have told her a few Chopper Read bedtime stories myself, but that would be taking things too far.

I didn't ask her what the fight was about as I was trying to remember the way to a small side lane that ran off another side lane. I was trying to find an old Chinese gambling club Mad Charlie had introduced me to in 1974, and I wondered if it was still going. It had been going since the 1920s and had been run by Mama San for the past twenty years – thirty years, really, but like most ladies she lies about her age.

Yes, the lady in charge had been in control of Chinese gambling for the past thirty years. A woman with fourteen sons doesn't need to be a man, now that's a bit of Chinese wisdom that puts Irish logic to shame.

I located the club in question only to find it had been turned into a whore house and Mama San was up at the Crown Casino with everyone else. I was dumbfounded. Why doesn't the National Trust save what really matters? Mamma San's, Bojangles nightclub and a half a dozen old-style massage parlours from the seventies, for instance. But we can't live in the past I suppose.

I walked back toward the Le Meridien filled with my own thoughts of the Melbourne I had lost when I realised that young Monique was still walking beside me, chattering away. 'Up here isn't a bad place, Chopper.' Monique darted through a dark doorway and up a flight of stairs past a big bald bouncer who tried to tell me that I knew his mother. I smiled, nodded and walked on by hoping to hell that I didn't know his mother – or, if I did, that she had hair and wasn't sixteen stone at the time.

The club was dark as all clubs are. Some chick tried to take my overcoat.

'May I take your coat, sir?' she asked.

'No, you may not take my coat,' I replied.

Within moments the manager of the club was notified. Evidently there was a no-eared gentleman in the club who would not surrender his overcoat to the overcoat lady. I did not know that this was now illegal in Melbourne but I had been away a long time. The manager was a little, very polite, very nice Chinese lady.

'Hello, I am manager, how may I help you? You frighten girl when you no give her coat, she think you have gun.'

Who could think of such a thing? As though I have ever used an overcoat to conceal weapons. The very thought of it is just spooky.

The bouncer was in some sort of nervous state, but the Chinese manager soon got with the programme.

'When they tell me Chopper Ree here I have to come say hello.'

'Read,' I said, 'not Ree.' I hate to be a stickler for diction, but we have to do our best.

She smiled and said, 'Chopper Ree.'

I nodded and smiled back. 'Yes, Read.'

'You drink at bar, no pay,' said the little Chinese lady. She called a girl over and said, 'Mr Chopper Ree no pay.' I looked around the club and half the place seemed to have mobile phones stuck to their ears. None of these peanuts were talking on mobile phones when I came in and they weren't ringing dial-a-prayer.

I polished off a few free drinks and walked out noticing that the door bouncer had totally vanished, not a bad trick for a slob as big as him. Shit, maybe I did know his mother, but I'm pleased to say not too well, as her bouncing baby boy doesn't look like me at all. As I walked down the street I heard the sound of high heels against cement. Young Monique was running after me.

'Hang on, Chopper, where you going?' she asked.

'Back to my hotel,' I replied.

'Great.' She smiled wide. 'Let's rock on.'

I don't think I misunderstood her. I was old enough to be her dad but not so old that I didn't pick up the thread of the conversation.

'Nah, Princess,' I said. 'My wife is waiting for me. She's having a baby in September, it's late and she will be wondering where I am. I gotta go.'

And with that I turned and walked away.

'See you, Chopper,' came the voice. I knew I wouldn't.

All I wanted to do was get back to the hotel and see Mary-Ann, then get on a plane and get out of Melbourne. I returned to the Hotel Le Meridien (which means rip-off in French) and Mary-Ann was waiting for me. A little annoyed, a little worried but glad to see me. We went to bed, but I couldn't sleep.

FOR some reason I kept thinking how I hadn't seen Flinders Street Station at night. I tossed and turned but couldn't sleep. It was 4am. I got up and got dressed. I was going out. But this time Mary-Ann wasn't going to be left in a hotel room, so she got up and got dressed as well and we took off for an early-morning walk around the old home town. I knew I may never be back and I wanted one last look.

We must have walked for miles but as we walked past the drunks, junkies, vomit and blood of Saturday night and Sunday morning in Melbourne, all I wanted to do was go back to Richmond, Tasmania, and kiss every blade of grass on the farm. We had both changed, me and Melbourne, and we no longer recognised each other. I was a stranger. It made me realise that a man can only march forward, he can never go back. I felt sad. I'd spent quite a few years missing my old home town only to find that my Melbourne had gone.

My memory of it was alive, but all else was dead. I wondered at the young, big-eyed kid who had followed me about hours before. When I tell people I've been walking around town with Chopper Read they won't believe me, she said. Poor old Chopper Read, I thought to myself, he is alive and well inside the imaginations of others, but for me that Mark Brandon Read is also just a memory that goes with my old Melbourne. A long-ago memory.

We walked back to the hotel and dozed a bit before room service brought up our breakfast. Warm ham, warm bacon, warm snags, warm tomato, warm eggs, toast and hot coffee. The coffee was good. The food wasn't as good as a Pentridge prison breakfast on Christmas Day. Especially when I took all the sausages one time. Ha, ha.

All in all, the bloody Meridien needs to lower its prices and lift its game. Also I am told a writer isn't a real writer till he gets to slag off at least one five-star hotel and restaurant. I couldn't even be bothered to pinch the towels.

We returned to Tasmania and, as far as I am concerned, I won't leave the island again unless money is involved, and lots of it.

Postscript to the Polish screw from Pentridge: Monique was a bloody nice kid, a little on the wild side and just a touch crazy but, as I remember, so were you. And no, mate, in case you're wondering, everything in this story is true. I did not plonk your daughter, I maintained my gentleman status at all times. You were kind to me in there, mate, and many years later I returned the favour. We're even – via con dios amigo.

DON'T ever go shopping with your wife. I needed some new underpants. I'm now tipping the scales at a dainty eighteen stone. I waited outside the store trying to act debonair and Mary-Ann selected several pairs of extra extra large jockey-type underpants.

The sales girl and her various sales-lady friends gathered as well as lady shoppers and held the offending garments up for inspection. Other ladies came over and inspected the underwear then Mary-Ann called me over. I had to walk through a small army of smiling girls, mothers, shoppers and sales ladies while the jumbo mansize lingerie was held up against my embarrassed person for further inspection. Ladies, girls, onlookers came from everywhere. Chopper Read was buying underpants. This was a must-see moment.

'These ones are nice,' said one lady, holding a pair of gentleman's bikini briefs up against me.

A small girl had run off to get some boxer shorts. Should I take the Bonds Jockeys or the Calvin Klein, as underpants were thrust at me and held up against me by various interested ladies?

'I just want a couple of sets of underpants,' I said. 'Big ones.' I was so embarrassed I would have bought anything to get out of there.

I turned and walked out, waiting in the street outside. Mary-Ann followed along having purchased two pairs of jumbo jockey shorts that could have doubled as circus tents. 'Don't take me shopping with you again,' I said. 'In future just get me big underpants, socks and T-shirts.'

I could not believe what she had just put me through. And I thought prison was bad.

CHAPTER 10

PSYCHICS FOR PSYCHOS

'I'm sorry. Chopper Read has left the stage and is just sitting in a chicken shed playing cards with Elivs. No guns allowed.'

OUR dog Little Bill went missing a while ago. Mary-Ann was in tears of great panic and concern. You would have thought he was one of the Beaumonts.

We drove all over the farm looking for Little Bill, then we went back home and while I continued to look Mary-Ann rang some psychic hotline and they told her the dog was down the main road a good mile from the house, so down we went. No Little Bill to be seen.

By this time Mary-Ann was beside herself, and home we went again. Mary-Ann made another phone call while I went walking around yelling, 'Billy, Billy.' I was taking the scientific approach.

The psychic told her the dog would be found within half an hour near water so I went down to the dam yelling 'Billy, Billy' and thinking about drowning a psychic, who charge about ten bucks a second to talk shit.

Then Mary-Ann yelled out, 'I found him.' The dog had been locked in the cupboard and was found standing in a puddle of his own piss. 'The psychic lady said he'd be found near water,' said Mary-Ann. And they call me a mentally-ill crim.

I tell this yarn while making no remark whatsoever re the mental health of either my darling wife or the lady psychic. I have to sneak away to write my book either late at night or early morning as living on a farm with farm duties and animals demanding attention, not to mention a wife who as sure as God made little green apples will call me after about ten minutes to attend to something or the other ...

She once called me away from my writing to come and see the way Poop Foot our cat was sitting. Do all great writers have to put up with this? No wonder Hemingway topped himself. At least he had a double-barrel shotgun to do it with.

THE parting of the ways has finally come for me and my dear old dad. I love my dad and I always will but his state of mind can no longer be tolerated.

'What that bastard needs, son, is a shot in the skull.' These are the words of fatherly advice I was always given in relation to any person that fell foul of my father, and for a gunman fresh out of prison living with a father who actively encourages his son to take up arms against enemies real or imagined this is not a mentally, emotionally or physically healthy state of affairs.

I am just about to become a dad myself as I write, so I spend more and more time thinking about it. I cannot promise to be the perfect father, but I know I will never encourage my boy to become a one-man urban army.

I have my 'unborn' son to consider. Little Charlie. When I told my dad of the news of Mary-Ann's pregnancy he rang the local newspaper. You see, my dad calls me 'Chopper', and sees himself as the father of a notorious Melbourne gunman. This is his status, this is how he sees himself. I no longer see myself as a notorious Melbourne gunman criminal or anything. I have retired, but my father cannot see it. Most fathers would be distressed that their only son turned out to be a gunnie, but my dad wears it as a badge of honour.

I am now a bloke that used to be a once was. I am trying my best to be something different and having a dad who won't let go of the old me can only end in grief. I am a farmer now, a middle-aged, fat farmer – and I like it. I'm the fat bloke in the white T-shirt, as the lady in the pub so correctly put it. But to my dad I will always be the gunnie, Chopper Read. I have grown up but he won't, which is a bit of a worry when you're in your seventies.

I haven't spoken to my father in well over six months. He has contacted everyone from the Minister of Police to Dave the Jew trying to get them to make me contact him.

I haven't seen Dave the Jew for the same reason. I love Dave and I always will but Dave only wants me to return to Melbourne and take up arms against enemies real and imagined.

Both Dad and Dave want me to live the legend, but I no longer wish to live that life. I did my twenty three years in prison. Dave the Jew should have been beside me, but I kept my mouth shut. All bills paid, Dave, and you too, dad.

I'm sorry, pop, but I've got my own little family to think about now. Chopper Read has left the stage and is just sitting in a chicken shed playing cards with Elvis. No guns allowed.

TWO young film makers, Frank Mirowski and Jason Carter, want to do a documentary on me, interviewed by Miss Nude Australia Alison Downes as per usual. I was pissed and told a heap of lies, but it's all good footage I'm sure.

Now they want me to do a keep-fit exercise video with 'Candy' Alison doing all the workout stuff wearing next to nothing while I sit by eating a pizza, hold the anchovies. Sounds good to me.

I took 'Candy' Alison along with me to meet a media-type person at the Wrest Point Casino. She was all teeth, tits and legs, but a bit nervous.

'What will I say to him?' asked Alison.

'Tell him that you have never met a guy you couldn't deep throat,' I replied.

Alison nodded in a serious manner.

I was kidding. I meant it was a joke, a laugh, I was having a giggle, not a gargle. Alison walks up, shakes his hand and tells him right out that she has never met a guy she couldn't deep throat.

The article was never printed in the national magazine. I wonder why. But the editor still rings me to ask after Alison's well being. Some people can take a joke, some people can't and some people shouldn't be joked with at all. So much for Australian men's magazines. And they say people buy them for the articles.

Now, Alison was just joking, for underneath it all she is quite prim and proper. The editor of the major men's magazine turns out to be a politically correct pansy. I mean the bloke nearly wet his pants with embarrassment … or something like that.

'Was it something I said?' asked Alison as I sent her home in a taxi. She really is quite innocent ... if you say that about a girl who spends her working days in a G-string sticking her bottom in other people's business.

CHAPTER 11

THE PREGNANT PAUSE

'If I rang Joe tomorrow and said, "Get on a plane and go and shoot whoever," it would be done. But why would an author want someone killed?'

ONE of my problems in writing a book at home is that I often find my wife Mary-Ann in an ill mood. Pregnant women are a beautiful thing, but you could get whiplash trying to keep up with the mood swings.

Sadly, when she should be concentrating on sleeping and getting bigger with our unborn son she decides to become a part-time literary critic.

I find that Mary-Ann has tiptoed in to have a sneaky read of what I have just written. This is not good. I have written some fairly hurtful things about various murderers, police, psychopaths and some who are all three (sorry, Denis), and have never had anything to worry about until I saw the look on my wife's face after she (without invitation) had a speed read through the manuscript.

Naturally, any comedy relating to my wife or mention of another female in sexual or comic tones is greeted with a certain frost. 'What's wrong, bubby?' I ask in a pathetic attempt to suck up.

'Nothing,' is the cool reply through clenched teeth. I then look and sure enough my pad and pen have been slightly moved.

'Have you been reading my book?' I ask.

'No, why would I want to read it?' comes an icelike reply.

I've come to realise that a married man takes his life in his hands page by page when writing a book at home. It's not easy work. Try it if you don't believe me. No wonder some authors go to garrets to punch out a good yarn – or they'd be punching on with their wives.

It ain't easy to write a bestseller with the missus looking over the shoulder after she's done the washing up.

My books have always been written taking the mood of others into consideration with each and every story involving a certain personal risk. There's the risk of offending either the person you are writing about or the person reading it. Oh well, play on. But just think about the sacrifices I make so that you can have a chuckle.

I CREATED a storm with my first book *Chopper from the Inside* (you didn't know I could write in italics, did you?) I told a lot of hard-to-believe true yarns and told stories about a lot of hard-to-believe real-life people. A lot of the men I named in my first book never lived to read my second – so, too, with the third and again with the fourth.

There are still a lot of blokes I'd love to write about, but only after they are dead. Playing with words to avoid a lawsuit isn't my cup of tea, but I'm sure everyone I want to die will die in time. Don't ask me why.

As I sit and write this a large black spider walks across the table. It's been raining outside. The spiders around here come inside when the weather gets bad. We even get spider webs inside the car. I moved a few books and so on and got up to kill it, but it vanished among my papers. My war with spiders started in prison, but I've now given up, so if they leave me alone I'll leave them alone. This is my new philosophy on hairy, disgusting, dangerous creatures, including former prison mates.

I hope this particular spider moves along as I recognise him as a venomous, dangerous-type bastard. It's quite unnerving so I will put my pen down and move along hoping that tomorrow he, too, has moved along *via con dios*. I'll make a deal, he doesn't try to bite me and I won't try to bite him. Seems fair to me.

I killed the spider. He walked right across the page. Ghandi may have shooed him away, but bugger that. I don't wear a turban and I don't drink my own piss in the morning.

I did not want to write about the joys of living with a pregnant woman as any man reading this who has had to live with a pregnant woman knows they get sick in the morning and we feel sick for the rest of the day. It is a delight indeed. The mood swings from happiness to tears.

I can cope with the 'don't come near me, it's all your fault that I'm fat and getting fatter' and the 'I hate you, get out of the house', the fits of rage and jealousy, temper, then the need to move furniture, the need to spend money on this, that and the other, the mental and emotional spin-outs and flip-outs, the fear and panic fits, then the love and happiness, then the taking every word you say apart and asking you what you really meant, then the what if the baby is born deaf, blind, deformed, dead? The SIDS, cot death, horror stories told to her by every woman who ever gave birth.

In between there is a lot of normality and love, but when the mood swings hit they hit like Frankie Waghorn, but with less warning. Pregnant ladies are, to say the least, unpredictable.

Even with cyclones there is normally a warning. Birds chirp before the rain, the sirens go off before the bombs drop, police sometimes say 'drop the gun' before they shoot you, although in Melbourne they mostly say it after. But when a woman is up the duff there is no warning when the wind is about to change.

One minute they are trying to lift something ten men would have trouble with, next minute they are lounged in a chair asking you to clean out the bird cage because she simply can't move.

Then there's the sleeping – or lack of it – and the getting up twenty times a night to go to the toilet. One minute life is dull and boring, next minute we are going out too much. It's a see-saw rollercoaster ride of pure emotion.

You can imagine I have learnt how to deal with the mentally unwell and violent types in prison but nothing prepares you for the pregnant woman.

I've got nothing to wear, she says suddenly, so new clothes are bought and three weeks later there's complaints of only having the same clothes to wear. Then she's offering me something to eat, and taking offence when I say no. The point being that if I eat then she can eat too.

Living with a pregnant woman? It has to be said it's like living with a sometimes friendly mental patient.

Of course, when this is read after the baby arrives all will be denied but I've spoken to other men who have lived with the Great Pregnant Emotional Monster and all the stories are basically the same. I've listed only a few, the list of mental and emotional mood swings is psychologically unbelievable.

I love you, I hate you, what do you want for breakfast? Get out of the house and never come back, do you think a blue or red rug for the hallway? All within an hour of getting out of bed. Then the day begins.

Holy shit, I will no doubt regret writing this but I believe it needs to be said.

Pregnancy involves hard labour for more than one person, believe me, and I've done a bit of hard labour over the years.

WE HAVE a septic tank toilet system at our place. One bathroom, two toilets, all very posh. But when it rains the toilets back up and I have to go out and remove the lid of the tank and start to bucket it out. Top job.

Someone uses a lot of toilet paper is all I can say. However, everything in married life is the man's fault so I get the blame for that as well. In the morning, I must light the fire in the kitchen for the cats, let the dog out and unlock and feed the chickens and chainsaw the wood, and hope you don't get it the wrong way around.

Then the one who walks on water will get up at around 9am, and say good morning with a big smile, ask have the cats been fed (yes), the budgies and canary fed (yes), and has Little Bill had morning walk, poo, piddle and breakfast? Yes again.

Then she will walk past the washing machine and shake hands with herself and start it up to celebrate.

Thus another day in paradise begins. Bloody wood cutting followed by emptying out a septic tank? Good morning to you too. And I fought to get out of jail for this.

I NOW have to wear glasses. The years of writing books in my cell in the dark by the light of the television have come back to haunt me. So now I'm the fat, middle-aged, alcoholic chicken farmer with glasses.

I'm also having driving lessons with the RAC. My driving instructor is Sharon Figg and she tells me I drive a car like a man trying to leave the scene of a crime. Ha, ha.

I have to get my licence so as to drive 'she who walks on water' into hospital and bring her home with our baby son, so it's quite serious. I've never bothered with a driving licence previously. I always found that when I jumped in a car carrying a large handgun the driver seemed happy to take me where I wanted to go.

I've lit the fire and collected the eggs. Life looks beautiful on a farm in the morning and as 'she who walks on water' snoozes I have a private moment of reflection. It is 6am.

What an arsehole, vicious, cold-blooded, savage, cruel, sadistic, psychopathic, gun-happy, mental case I was years ago. And they were my good points. I ran on pure high-octane ego but as I stand in the chicken shed with my eggs and Gladys and the girls looking up at me as if to say look at the good job we did, I don't hate a living thing.

I HAD a dream the other night that Leearna, the barmaid at the Richmond Arms, was mowing my lawn. I looked out the window and there was half the bloody hotel having a party at my place. It's these stupid nicotine patches that make me dream. I haven't had a smoke in eight weeks and right now I could smoke this biro.

These dreams keep returning. I don't know what it is with Leearna and my lawnmower but sure enough she was out there again last night.

I took the editor of *Ralph* magazine to a club for a drink and a feed and among other things got him to stick Natasha Downes, Alison's sister, in as Barmaid of the Month on page 131 of the April issue, 1999. OK, it may not be an Order of Australia, but it's a start. Mark Dapin, the editor of the magazine, had a good night out at my expense – free food, free booze and Shane Farmer turned the whole club on for the bloke.

I don't know what else he got, because I left before he did, but the bloke had a good time. If you were the editor of a national men's magazine at a lap-dancing club with the owner doing his best to make you happy I reckon you'd have a good time, too. Then again I could be wrong. I should have taken Mark Dapin to the Richmond Arms. Leearna would have made a much better barmaid of the month. She's my favourite barmaid, anyway. Anyone who visits you in your dreams and mows your lawn gets my vote. Next time, Leearna, what about painting the house?

I did Natasha Downes a big favour by asking Mark Dapin to stick her in as barmaid of the month and she hasn't had the good manners to show up in any of my dreams let alone mow my bloody lawn.

I am again digressing from the point. I have decided to make my own video. I will call it 'A Man and his Chainsaw'. I will begin tomorrow. As the reader will recall, I recently bought a timber lease from my father-in-law. Trees and plenty of 'em and all mine to cut down.

They may have taken my guns but the buggers won't get my chainsaw. And I have completed the appropriate course in Risdon prison, so I am an expert.

Now I think I might smoke a nicotine patch. Yummy.

MY old friend Frankie Waghorn wrote me a letter. He's doing a life sentence in prison up Beechworth way for the murder of that rat Johnny Turner. I still believe Frank didn't do it. He may have helped dispose of the mortal remains and steam clean the carpet, but that's only because Frankie was always house proud. Whoever imagined you could get life for a little spring cleaning? I don't believe for a moment Frank actually stabbed the little turd.

I never liked 'The Beeper' Johnny Turner, I never liked his old two-bob gangster uncle, Joey Turner, either – Jackie Twist's offsider. Killing any member of that wombat crew comes under the heading of a community service.

I don't hear much from old jail associates. Craig Minogue the Russell Street bomber don't write to me no more and Julian Knight, the Hoddle Street massacre man, don't write either.

I skip to the letter box every day but no mail from the mentally ill to the reformed mentally ill. I guess no one is much interested in the doings of a fat chicken farmer these days. Friendship is a funny business.

Most of my old friends are dead or in prison doing life and the new ones you make, well, it's just not the same. I'm still in touch with Joe Ditrola in South Australia and I've still got some good Albanian friends. If I rang Joe tomorrow and said, 'Joe, get on a plane and go and shoot whoever,' it would be done. But why would an author want someone killed?

Friendship these days is bullshit. It's all good-time stuff. You can't find hard-time friends. I've still got hard-time friends but they are growing fewer and fewer. On one hand I'm no longer part of the world I came from so I've had to say *adios amigos* to those blokes as their friendship means me going back to help fight their wars, real and imagined.

I'm a very torn man where friendship is concerned and I end up a ripped man when I go to the pub. I came from a world where you killed for your friends and they killed for you and now I'm in a new world mixing with people and calling people my friends knowing that if Mad Charlie came back to life tomorrow he'd spit on them and say, 'Chopper, what's going on?'

So now I guess I'm just a friendly person mixing with friendly people but in my heart I know that the people I smile at today wouldn't have got within three hundred yards of me ten years ago so I'm a man very, very much alone and without close friends in a world full of people saying, 'How you going, Chopper?'

Then I get the Chopper Read friends. These are the people who have read my books and have gotten friendly with me. I've had to knock a few of them on the head because their wives all wanted to do the business, which was a pity because the husbands weren't bad blokes at all.

I mean you invite people into your home or into your life under the heading of friendship and the husband gets pissed and tells you he's your best fucking mate and the wife gets pissed and wants you to shag her and when you tell the mad bastards to piss off they accuse you of being a snob.

The more I see of people the more I like my dog. There are a couple of stories I could tell relating to wives of really good blokes but if I named them or didn't alter a few key points the blokes in question would be doing jail time for kicking shit out of the mad cows.

Four stories really. I covered myself by alerting Mary-Ann right away but I will say that each wife made her sly move with her own husband not twenty feet away. Not a physical move, just a polite verbal whisper that I need not call a plumber if ever my main pipe got blocked up.

I mean this is dangerous stuff. Three of the four guys in question had heavy duty firearm collections. I mean I was sad to see them go, but back dooring Mary-Ann is a no no.

I've been through all that shit in previous relationships and always come undone.

Friendship, that's what I was originally on about. The great mystery word. It's like the word mateship. It was a word that meant something in Australia, now it's just an overused word meaning if you can be of use to someone then that someone will become your 'mate'.

Yes, there are exceptions and contradictions to every rule of law but, generally speaking, friendship and mateship is dead. Now it's all just a mass of smiling false pretenders all picking each other's pockets. Yeah, I'm an old jaded sceptic, but I'm not far wrong, am I?

I can no longer demand loyalty because the people who would give it are from my old world. I could never give it back. To these people it is blood loyalty and that means blood can and will be spilled. I cannot go back so I must accept my new good-time friends and say goodbye to the real hard-time mates.

I WAS sitting in the Brunswick Hotel in Liverpool Street, Hobart, the other day. It's owned by Butch Hudson, Peter Hudson's brother, as in the former Hawthorn great who could shoot almost as straight as me. It was there that I bumped into this cross-eyed chick.

Now, as a rule you don't run into many cross-eyed girls and when you do they sort of stand out in your memory and it reminded me of cross-eyed Sharon – or Clarence as we used to call her. Don't get me wrong, Sharon may have been cross-eyed but she never crossed her legs. They were permanently open to suggestion.

The expression 'every man and his dog' comes to mind when I think of Sharon. OK, I'm a bit one-eyed in my view of the woman. After all, she did try to sink me on a murder charge but picture this, if you will, a cross-eyed prostitute with a great body, and I mean model material.

She had all the goodies in all the right places, it's just that the chick was cross-eyed. This girl had one eye looking at the other and neither of 'em looking at you.

She had to wear glasses but would not wear them so when she was working she was as blind as a bat. Now brothels aren't brightly lit places. Dim lighting is the order of the day (or night) and you had this chick who was so blind she would stab herself in the eye when she went down on you.

It was like rolling about with Mr Magoo – if Mr Magoo looked like Jane Fonda.

All the boys knew her. She was famous. I mean rolling up to a function with a cross-eyed whore was considered quite a giggle round my neck of the woods. She was also a junkie and really loved her heroin.

Now, to some of you who don't understand the ways of the underworld, let me explain. Prostitutes who love heroin and don't like to pay for it – well, they get screwed a lot. So crossed-eyed Sharon was more than famous, she was a legend.

She came to visit me in 1984 when I was in Geelong prison and you guessed it, I fell in love. I know love can be blind, but in this case it was cross-eyed. The chick blew in, blew me, and blew out again. Who says romance is dead?

What chance did I have? I'd been in jail a long time, I was seeing Margaret at the time but I was a greedy bastard. I also had Tracey Warren and a few others popping in to see me.

I mean when you're twenty nine years old you just don't worry about that sort of shit.

None of these girls were waiting for me with their legs nailed to the floor, I mean when some of your lady friends (not Margaret, of course, she was respectable) are working in brothels looking over their shoulder saying to the bloke humping them, 'I'm Chopper Read's girlfriend,' it is hardly *Breakfast at Tiffany's,* is it?

So don't be too unkind in your thinking in relation to my past jailhouse love life. Anyway, back to cross-eyed Sharon. This chick was a sexual public toilet with the body of a beauty queen and providing she wore her dark glasses or you didn't look her in the eye, all was well.

Anyway, I wanted to get Sharon a diamond ring so I rang Mad Charlie and asked him to go around to Sharon's place with a diamond ring. 'Not another girlfriend, Chopper,' he said. 'Jesus, give it a rest.' But Charlie went around and gave her the diamond ring and then came in to visit me.

'Hey, Chopper, have you had a good look at this chick?'

'What's wrong, Charlie?' I asked.

'Well,' replied Charlie, 'apart from being a prostitute and a junkie, the fucking moll is cross-eyed.'

'Yeah,' I said, 'but she can suck the chrome off an exhaust pipe.' I felt it was gallant of me to defend her in such a way.

'She'd fucking need to,' snarled Charlie, 'she'd starve to death otherwise.' He always was a romantic, being European and all.

Charlie had a blunt way of putting things, but he was quite right. I got out of prison and had a good close look at Sharon. There was no nice way to put it, her life was parked in a handicapped zone. That's what jail can do. Frogs start to look like princesses. Sharon ended up with Nick the Greek for a while. The cross-eyed give-up junkie maggot got passed around like the only toilet roll at a footy match and I thought I was in love with it. I wasn't. It was all part of the prison madness that grips the hearts and minds of only the lonely.

THE last time I saw my mate Shane Farmer and his girl, Alison Downes, Shane wanted me to invest in some lap-dancing club in South Yarra and Alison said she needed to see a psychiatrist.

I don't know if either was serious. Nightclub people are nice people but they all live in their own strange twilight zone. I think the lack of natural light eventually starves the brainbox.

I've known a lot of nightclub owners and they are all carbon copies of each other. They stagger from rich to poor, from diamonds to broken glass, in an after-dark world of make believe.

They live like millionaires and movie stars in a world of dreams and strobe lighting and, like vampires, they come to life at night. There have been a few of them that I have threatened with a wooden stake (and a couple with sawn-off shotty as well).

Every club owner and dancer I've met could write their own book if they could sit still long enough to do it, which they couldn't.

They live in a three-dimensional nervous breakdown. After a while I've got to just walk away before I get invited too deeply into the madness they live in.

I used to know a guy named Athol. He ran more nightclubs and knew more about nightclubs than anyone in Melbourne. Mad Charlie introduced me to him.

The bloke has made and lost millions. In the end he got swallowed up by the monster he created. His whole life was night time, loud music, and strobe lighting.

If you invest in one nightclub you invest in a sort of make-believe madness. Booze, drugs, girls, music – it's like you have bought yourself your own private slice of Hollywood, then you hock your arse and your first investment to the bank to re-invest in a second club, bigger and better, and the rollercoaster begins. In the end you're a nightclub boss worth a million on paper, driving a leased Lamborghini living in a leased million-dollar home with a leased girlfriend, renting a penthouse in Surfers Paradise with a lifestyle costing you thousands a day, borrowing more and more money to buy a slice of bigger and better clubs.

Why do they do it? Well, they have to get the new club because the punters are so fickle. Every cool spot ends up being uncool. The crowd moves on and the owner is left with a couple of empty club dunnies full of spew and a few ecstasy tablets on the floor. They have to try and anticipate what the crowd wants and provide it before they even know they want it. It stands to reason that eventually they will zig when they should have zagged and come a gutser. They want the A crowd in their club to get the drongos to come in as well. Can you think how much Scotch and Southern Comfort they've poured down the gullets of bit-part actors, TV hacks and pissed sportsmen just to create that 'in crowd' feeling?

If nightclub owners had any actual cash we would have been kidnapping them years ago. Ha, ha. Invest money in a nightclub? Forget it. I'd rather invest in a pay toilet. You don't have to put strobe lights in a dunny. Most of the nightclub mob are good people, great to talk to, with a thousand stories, but in the end it's the twilight zone.

When I was a gunnie years ago, club owners were all part of the action, and the girls that went with that life. It was all bullshit, bullets and big tits. Maybe I'm getting older and wiser, or maybe I've just seen too much, I don't know.

I've got to stop writing now. Poop Foot my cat doesn't like writing and when he has had enough he jumps up on the table and sits on the pad so I must leave the hefty and unanswered question of nightclubs and nightclub owners alone for now. When a cat puts its arse on your masterpiece you wonder whether he is voting with Mary-Ann to say it's a pile of crap.

Via con dios, Amigos.

CHAPTER 12

DEATH IS A FUNNY BUSINESS

'There are only nine year-in, year-out hitmen in Australia today ...'

DEATH is a funny business and the very, very few people who deal in death for dollars are themselves a funny lot. There aren't as many professional hit men about as the police, media and popular television hacks would have you believe. But the world is full of killers. Everyone can kill if pushed. Even you, dear reader, sitting there looking into a world of death and blood through the pages in this book. You probably think you could never enter the world of the Chopper Reads. Think again. It only takes someone to push the right (or wrong) button and everyone can go off until the object of hatred is no longer breathing.

So let us not mix up common or garden murder, or the act of murder, with an execution. I want to talk about the professional hitman, not a once-only mug who got paid to kill another mug and got caught and then rests himself and his wombat reputation in prison.

As a hitman, I mean a real true blue, regular as clockwork, thirty on the scoreboard over a twenty-year period and not so much as a fucking parking ticket. That sort. By the way, there were never more than a dozen of them in Australia and Chris Flannery never even got a mention. Just because you get put off by a hitman don't mean you are one.

There are only nine year-in, year-out hitmen in Australia today and they are all friends or friends of friends and can, if need be, reach each other.

Straighter shooters … my music manager Colin Dix (*above*) and bodyguard Dean Petrie (*left*).

Next to Mary-Ann these are my favourite girls … Alison Downes (*left*) and barmaids Monique (*above*) and Leearna (*right*).

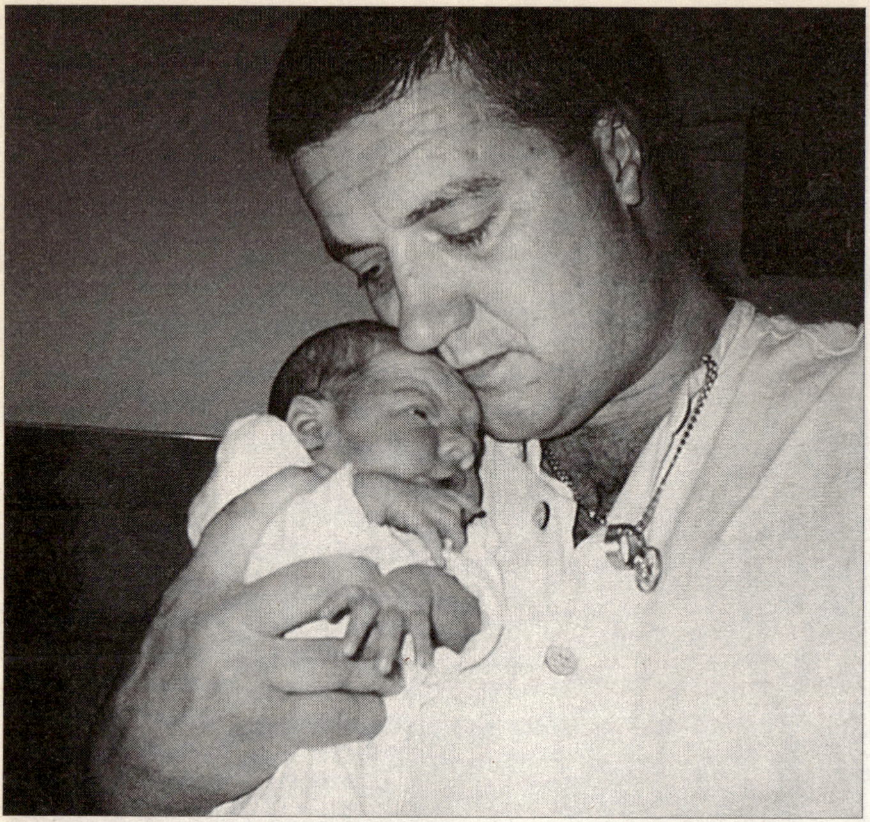

Right: Mad Charlie shot dead. I named my son (*above*) after him.

The lovely Mary-Ann.

Dinner and a date. I hate sheep but love Watchchook.

Top: The Chopper Read fan club.

Above: It's surprising what you can bury under wood.

Honey, I'm home.

Nine year-in, year-out full-on hitmen and four gunsmiths between the nine of them, and the gunsmiths get their guns from one of three sources. So, all in all, between hitmen, gunsmiths and suppliers you have a network of sixteen men in all.

Each hitman may be part of a crew, a team, or yes, even a gang. Let's say a bike gang for example. (Now, dear reader, that might be a hint.)

However, their loyalty to their gunsmith overrides their loyalty to their crew, team or gang. What am I trying to say? Am I trying to tell you something? Is the fat bloke in the white T-shirt hinting at something, maybe that I may predict certain things before they even happen? Then again, how could I possibly do that? I'm just a fat chicken farmer who spends his days stuffing chooks rather than drug dealers.

No one needs pay any attention to my insane ranting and ravings, do they? So let's get hypothetical. What would a bloke do if, for example, he heard about something that was to go off on or around the time of the Olympic Games?

Let's just say that a fortune teller wrote a book and in that book the fortune teller predicted the death of a person. Where does the fortune teller stand legally? But what if the fortune teller happens to be a former hardcore, heavy duty criminal with almost military-type connections relating to the sale of illegal small-arms ordinance? Now, if a fortune teller of that calibre was to make a prediction or give advance warning, a futuristic forecast based, let's say, on a dream, then how would that place him legally?

We are talking about a fortune teller who has no interest at all in being questioned over anything. Gee, I bet that fortune teller could, for example, sell a hell of a lot of books if he was to write a book and name names ... but would the profit be worth the fucking headache? I don't think so.

Anyway, a fortune teller who gets it right could be considered someone who had knowledge of a crime prior to the commission of that crime. Personally, I don't think it would be a very smart thing at all for a fortune teller to make any rash predictions such as telling someone to check under the front seat before they start the car.

NOW this is a game called hypothetical and just to add legal safety to the yarn let's use the word theoretical. And considering the state of mind of the author let's throw in another word – certifiable.

A hypothetical Italian gent in South Australia, an old guy, very powerful in the Australian Italian criminal world, with relatives in Italy and America, is playing a game of cards with a younger Italian.

We will call the old Italian Paul and the younger one John or maybe Joe, OK? So now we begin the most wild and fantastic hypothetical yarn.

If you wanted to kill a famous person where would you do it? Not a political person and not a political event, but someone with more power than any politician and more fucking money. Easy, you'd pick a major sporting or entertainment event.

All the security is trained on the politicians, leaving big gaps in other security areas. The arrogance of politics is that politicians think they are the only worthwhile targets in the world when really no one cares apart from the IRA. Anyway, back to the hypothetical. Let's say there was a very very powerful man, a billionaire – no, not Kerry Packer, but another one.

What if he has stood on toes for years and two men, just as rich, or even a little richer, decided to fight back.

You can't break him by taking his money so how can you hurt him? You kill his number-one son. Yes, kill his son and shatter the enemy.

Psychological attack: kill the son.

It is easy enough to enter Australia to attend major sporting events such as the Melbourne Grand Prix, the Melbourne Cup, tennis events, big yacht races, and to avoid all counter-surveillance and anti-terrorist, protective security police and private firms. Carlos, The Jackal, could walk around the Melbourne Cup with a bazooka strapped to his back and the coppers would think he was a drunk public servant in some stupid fancy-dress gear.

The son has no security. However, it is taken for granted that his father sees to the son's personal security without the son even knowing it. Nothing is left to chance. Perhaps the son's interest in a certain Australian yacht race could be the best way of attack.

You can put a bodyguard on a yacht but that's about it. The logistics of full and total protection for a man floating on water are limited, to say the least.

But you can't use a skin diver and you can't stick a bomb under the yacht.

The son's security provided by dear old Dad have thought of that, hence a phone call to a fat bloke in the white T-shirt. This is not for sure, Chopper, this is just a question, they say. A theoretical question, I reply. Yeah, a theoretical question. In my (old) business I have seen more people end up dead from theoretical questions than anything else. 'If you wanted to blow up a boat with all the high-tech surveillance systems, I mean this kid had security up the arse, very hard to hit, how would you go about it?'

'Is this for real?' I asked.

'No, no, it's just a question. I'm having a debate with old Paul about how you could do this. General chit-chat and hypothetical story told over the phone. No one has asked anyone to kill anyone but money is floating about for ideas, ways and means. I don't know what's going on but I got a five-grand sling just to ring you,' said Joe.

'Why?' I asked.

'Because you're the only one who can reach the Jew or who could put it together. The only one I know, anyway,' he says. 'I told Paul you could fix it. Not that anything needs to be fixed. I'm only telling you what Paul told me,' said Joe. 'Fuck knows what drugs he's taking but the money's real. All they want is a good idea. These wombats will pay big money for a good idea, a good plan. No one is gonna get killed. All they want is like a plot, a movie. If you was gonna do it, how would you do it?' he asked.

'Ring me back tomorrow, Joe. Let me think this over.'

Why they would ask a chicken farmer such questions is another question but I am a warm sort of fellow so I am always ready to help out. After all, knowledge (and a 9mm pistol) is power.

I sat and considered this theoretical, hypothetical situation without being told who the so-called target was.

Enough was said in code for me to lock into the target.

Yacht race? Well, you wouldn't do it at the start in Sydney. You'd do it at the finish in Hobart. Now, a torpedo would be the only way.

Once the yacht was anchored. Now I don't have a torpedo but I know how to make one, as I'm sure most chicken farmers would ... one large oxygen cylinder, a fist full of plastic explosive and a small APM landmine.

Oxygen bottles float and they have parties on yachts at night.

The whole thing could be put into the water from a speed boat or rubber boat and pushed toward the yacht at a distance of twenty to sixty yards.

To be on the safe side use two. A big push and floating with the current, one home-made torpedo gently floats along.

Anything more than a gentle tap and vabooommm, up she goes.

It's so simple, like most bombs. Of course, I could not swear to the safety of the bloke in the rubber boat or speed boat. Now you would have to wire up the plastic. I won't go into detail. Other advice tells me I wouldn't need to.

I've fired a .303 round into plastic explosive at a hundred yards and nothing happened. It needs a detonator and a charge to explode it. The way it is put together is not the guts of the story. The guts of this yarn was the fact that very serious people had been contacted in relation to the hypothetical murder of this man.

The fact that I've even written this much means it will never happen. Isn't it weird? I've probably just saved his life.

CHAPTER 13

THE PEN IS MIGHTIER THAN THE SAWN-OFF

'I'm waiting for Jason and Nick the Greek to get murdered, as I'd rather write about them after they're dead.'

MY cousin, Geoff Pepper, reminded me that in all my books I've failed to mention that on the first and one and only time we ever got together I got him locked up for the night. We were on a train bound for a party at Box Hill. Me, Nick the Greek Apostolidis and about thirty sharpies. There was some fight and I got my long-haired hippy motorbike-riding cousin from Western Australia locked up. Nag, nag, nag. Why haven't I mentioned it before? OK Geoff, you're in the bloody book at long last and, yes, it's true that poor Geoff got arrested and locked up for the night simply for being in my company.

It was all my fault. I'm very sorry, it won't happen again. One night out in 1974 and he's never forgotten it. I mean, it was hardly the Great Bookie Robbery but now Geoff will want a walk-on part in *Chopper, The Movie*.

If there are any other relatives out there that I somehow got arrested twenty five years ago on some drunk and disorderly charge, consider yourselves noted but not mentioned, OK. Geoff, it was one night in the Box Hill lock-up not twenty five years on Devil's Island. So to Peppy and all the boys at Fletchers Harvey Hotel in Western Australia, *adios amigos*.

Right, now I've done all the cheerios, let's move along.

This book is taking me ages to write. It's easy in prison. You're locked in a cell with nothing to do but write. On the outside things take a lot longer. When you are writing there are two things you don't need, a wife and a dog, because they both expect your full attention.

I don't know if my books are getting better or getting worse but I've noticed people who worry about that sort of shit don't seem to sell a whole lot.

Like my publishers said to me, if we try to take it all to bits and figure out what makes it all work we will never be able to put it back together again, so to hell with it. I'll just keep on writing them and why you keep on reading them ain't none of my concern. Ha ha ha.

EVERY time I near the end of another book I wonder if it is to be my last. I've written fact, then fiction, now I'm back to fact. Admittedly I've played with some of the names, dates and places in this one so as to protect myself from the facts and from the guilty.

People have no sense of humour and as a chicken farmer I don't want to have to lawyer up and march back into court because some brain-dead goombah wants to have a go for defamation.

That is the trouble with being an author. The people you put in the books bleed because you have spoken of them and the people you don't write about crack the sads because they reckon they are worth a chapter or two. You can't win.

I just try to tell a tale which lets people know what is really happening when they turn their lights out to go to sleep. Even after nine books, I am still a raw beginner at this game. Most authors are faggot, junkie, art graduates with a government grant and understanding parents. I'm just a retired gunnie with no idea whatsoever but I suspect that when the socially radical and the would-be intellectuals want to go out and buy a book they find it hard to cop anything written by a bloke with no ears.

Some bloke in a black T-shirt puts rings through his ears and a stud through his tongue and they call that art. I wear a white T-shirt and have no ears and I'm called a freak.

You work it out.

They get a little tattoo on their stringy arms and they are making a statement. I have 'I love Ita Buttrose' on my arse and I am prescribed medication.

Love me or hate me, I've got the politically correct of this world totally screwed. Bad boy made good from the wrong side of the tracks. I was about to quote the famous words of a famous man who wrote a really famous book but I've forgotten who he was or the book he wrote but if you walked up to a drunk in a pub in the outback of Western Australia or the Territory or anywhere in this land they will either have read my books or would have heard my name, and a lot of them will try to tell you a Believe It Or Not, UFO Chopper Read story.

So to the lah de dah literary world, I piss on you all. Except, I fear, some of you would enjoy the odd golden shower. Like it or not, a hundred years after we are all dead most of you will be forgotten and I'll still be remembered.

Arrogant arsehole, aren't I?

It gives me little joy but I know it gives you pricks much pain. To all my critics with love, signed Chopper.

The bloke who can't spell, haunting you all with rows of books lined up in every airport bookshop. You people worry about the words while I worry about the story. You have to make it up because you don't know the truth. Wearing a nipple ring doesn't make you a tough guy.

GENE Autry once said that he was the first of the singing cowboys. Maybe not the best, but the best don't matter if you're the first.

Edmund Hilary may not have been the greatest rock climber and bee keeper God ever stuffed guts into, but he climbed the big one before the glorified tourists started queuing up to do it.

I'm probably not the best crook to write a book but I started it in these parts and, well, that's what counts. I might not touch a reader like George Orwell or Graham Greene could but I bet you I could bring tears to their eyes if I got the blow torch going on the soles of their feet.

I thought I might run short of things to write about now we are on the ninth book but I have discovered something that hack crime reporters have known for years. Crims keep on getting knocked off, and then you can talk about them. The difference is I know all of them and don't have to sit in a press conference being told lies by a copper who is waiting for some scientist from forensic to read the tea-leaves to guess what might have happened.

I'm waiting for Jason and Nick the Greek Apostolidis to get

murdered as I'd rather write about them after they are dead, that way I can't be sued for slander. It is just a matter of time before I can start to sharpen my pencil, because the dogs are barking.

I'm not calling publicly for anyone to shoot anyone, naturally, but it's a bit hard on a poor bloke trying to write a book without the benefit of a literary grant if people aren't being murdered fast enough.

I mean, for God's sake, what's the hold-up? I'd like Jason and Nick to both know that my pen is poised awaiting their exits, with a certain literary glee. Ha ha ha.

Don't lose your sense of humour, boys. I'm only being comic. I wish both Nick the Greek and young Jason the very best, although there's a lot to be said for euthanasia. All I'm saying is that from a writer's point of view it's a damn sight easier to write about people after they are dead. It saves a host of legal hassles. The blokes I want to write about just aren't dying fast enough. Get a wriggle on fellas. Haven't you heard the old gangster motto, live fast and die young?

TIGER Besanko is another one who should take a good, hard look at where his life is going and how it's interfering with my true-crime writing. C'mon, Tiger, get with the programme. When you're dead I'll make you famous from a literary point of view. There are blokes out there living far too bloody long.

Would it be asking too much for me to call on Jason, Nick Apostolidis and possibly Gilbert Besanko to commit suicide? Your deaths won't be in vain, I promise you. Come on, Nick, you're not doing much these days. You may as well be dead. Ha ha ha.

How am I meant to write a ripping good yarn about people without being sued? It's like pop stars. As soon as they neck themselves with a hard-on they sell a million records. I would have thought they would have sung better when they were alive.

If the buggers won't die on me, well, I'll just live in hope. Who knows, some nice reader might go out into the night and whack all three of you just to aid a poor struggling no-eared author. It's a strange world we live in, yes indeed. It really is.

What's that about the pen being mightier than the sawn-off?

Wouldn't it be funny if, in years to come, people found out that a certain unnamed literary person aided and planned the deaths of others simply because he wanted to write about them in his books without being sued. Yes, you're quite right. The whole topic is simply too far fetched. That would make a good plot for a wild crime-fiction movie, wouldn't it? The author and the hitman. They could call it *Chopper and the Jew,* maybe.

The hitman calling on the author to twist the facts ever so slightly in the direction of others so that he could continue to stand in the shadows. In return, the author calling on the hitman to once in a while, now and again, toss a little inside information his way or indeed whack one or maybe even two for the sake of a ripping read. Imagine that, an author who knew of a hit before it took place. Goodness gracious me.

No, you're quite right, the whole thing is too far fetched. An author working hand in hand with a hitman, indeed. Even Quentin Tarantino wouldn't touch a plot like that. Then again, Tarantino has been catching the late train to work on the Hitchcock Railway for a long time.

Think about it. One ear cut off 22 October 1990, in *Reservoir Dogs,* but ears had already fallen in another place on the other side of the world more than ten years before he ever thought of it. Imagine trying to out Chopper the Chopper – I should be paid royalties by that clown. Ha, ha.

I think I'd best leave this topic alone or certain paranoid people might start to think I'm not being comic and sarcastic, that this is not just a little bit of fun with words.

Perish the thought that anyone might feel for a moment I may be serious. I'm sure long lives will be had by all. Anyway, what the hell would I know? That's my story and I'm sticking to it.

MIDDLE-aged men who still view themselves as forces to be reckoned with, criminally speaking, bore me to tears. Age and wisdom cannot enter the field of criminal combat against the strength and madness of youth, although I must say that among the criminal youth of today I see no real threats. Once every ten to twenty years a real nutter comes along, so when the criminal history of Australia is written every hundred years there would only be five to ten names that would be worth the mention.

The rest would flow down the great steaming river of vomit out into the septic tank of nothingness where they belong and rightfully so. I'm rarely wrong in my criminal judgement of people and that's what kept me alive over the years but now and again I'm forced to reconsider my original opinion.

The old Collingwood saying of 'Good blokes don't get bail' comes back to haunt me. When I hear news of a so-called good bloke getting bail on a serious charge of robbery or violence I quietly wonder why some men are granted bail while the vast majority of offenders charged are left to rot in the remand yard. A case in point I'm forced to make mention of is my old mate Micky Marlow.

I wrote about Michael John Marlow in my second book *Chopper 2: Hits and Memories,* and if you haven't got it then get back to the book shop you tight-arsed bastard, and get it. Get the whole set as a matter of fact. I need the money, if my publishers don't drink all the profits.

Anyway, I digress. Years ago Micky was a good crook and a rock-solid crim. He was always a bit of a ladies man. I knew the bloke as a safe cracker, a tank man, a cool-headed professional.

Mick avoided prison because he was a thinker. I mean, he did a few months in the can but nothing worth a mention. He had been questioned over and over again relating to jobs all over Tasmania and the mainland, including murder. He was a chap I respected to a certain degree. One of my shortcomings is that I don't fully truly respect any crim who has not done the hard yards in the hard yards inside.

Good crims don't get bail and it's a prejudice of mine that dubious bastards never do much jail. I don't believe in good luck and active crims who continue to avoid prison are, in my opinion, suspect as it simply cannot continue without police help.

People who get bail and keep out of jail are usually the ones who keep talking to the police. In other words, they fill the jails with other people so they can stay outside. They stay out as long as they are useful to the coppers.

When I got out of prison I was contacted by Kellie, Micky's former *de facto* and the mother of his daughter. She wanted to see me. I wanted no part of it. I don't involve myself in interpersonal matters.

Kellie had given Micky the arse after finding Micky with another lass who looked rather similar. Typical Mick Marlow and highly comic, I thought. Mick was also still involved with a highly dubious collection of fellows I no longer wanted to hear about or know about.

If I wasn't going to see my own father because I considered him a security risk I could hardly see Micky. Then bang, Micky got pinched on a rape charge and got bail. A violent sex attack and bailed to appear. Sorry, but while I wish no one any ill will I don't want them sitting in my lounge room either.

Who gets bail on a rape charge? Certainly no one I know nor would want to know. God bless you and keep you all the best and all the rest but *via con dios, amigo*.

I have had a few mates pinched on rape, Mad Charlie included, but none of 'em ever got bail. Only certain types of people get bail and I'd rather not mix with them.

Call me a snob if you like. I got a $500 bail once in my life, in 1974, the result of a police clerical error after the Magistrate had formally refused bail.

I mean, sorry, but you gotta be a dead-set suckhole to get bailed on a serious charge. Yes, most people can get bailed with a top lawyer and a lot of bullshit but bashing women has never been my go and I don't go out of my way to mix with people who do.

Lions don't mix with hyenas. Bashing women in front of children, Jesus Christ. Anyway, I'm not trying to set myself up as some Alan Jones type moral judge, but Mick got eight years from a judge, which makes his pleas of innocence sound a little hollow.

I would have liked to give him the benefit of the doubt but Mick was convicted of rape – twice. Once could be a mistake, but twice is stretching it. To me it is most embarrassing to know that a former friend could sink so low. He had the money to pay for whores. Why bash and rape women? I simply cannot understand it.

He had a beautiful *de facto* and a couple of girlfriends on the side and he goes out and rapes some innocent country girl and beats her half to death.

I can't explain it. I have sat and watched men die, get shot or jailed. If you sit long enough by a river you will see all your enemies float past – face down.

I'm not saying everyone I know is a good bloke. I know some nice dead-set dogs. That's fine. I know they are dogs and so do they. No one is pretending to be what they are not, besides a good dog is worth his weight in gold, providing he isn't chewing on your leg and owns a few nightclubs. In Melbourne, not Hobart, I hasten to add. I cast no aspersions at nightclub people in Tasmania who may slip me the odd drink card.

But I digress. I guess I'm trying to say goodbye, Micky. You were one of the best, mate. Past tense. *Via con dios, amigo.*

FEW criminals ever walk out of the shadow of darkness and on into the light of normality. Most remain where they are or rise to a certain level then fall back. Few ever climb out of the sewer pit. I've walked through the shadow of the valley of death and I've no time or patience or pity for former colleagues who point blank refuse to march forward.

If this is a hard and unsympathetic attitude so be it but I'm not running some public charity operating a life-line for losers. As I've said before, *Je ne regrette rien*: I regret nothing.

It's high time a few of the so-called hard boys remembered this and stopped crying on every bastard's shoulder. As Billy Joe fell to the floor the crowd all gathered round and wondered at his final words. 'Don't take your guns to town, son, leave your guns at home, Bill, don't take your guns to town.'

You can laugh and you can cry, you can bleed until you die but one way or the other, son, your gonna pay your bill.

Postscript: Micky Marlow might possibly be the longest serving recipient of unemployment benefits in Australian history. In fact, no one I know can remember a time when Mad Micky was not collecting the dole. I think he went straight from kindergarten to the dole office. Do not pass go, do collect $100. I could be wrong. However Micky Marlow does recall to mind the old poem by A.B. 'Banjo' Paterson:

'Oh, it's dreadful to think in a country like this with its chances for work and enjoyment,
That a man like McGuinness was certain to miss whenever he tried for employment.'

And now, some Henry Lawson to go with it:

'And them that thinks they are better than the rest of all mankind while the sun never sets on the empire in their mind.'

Lawson wrote that about the Australian landed gentry squatter class.

He also noted that when the man from the city robs you he will do it with a gun at your head or a blade at your throat and have the manners to wear a mask, whereas the man from the bush will do it with a firm handshake and a warm smile.

I'VE always meant to include at least one recipe, ingredients and directions for the making of a particular Chopper dish in each book but never got around to it.

There are some really good ways of serving cheap cuts of stewing meat, lamb or beef. It don't matter. I call it Chopper's Hot Pot. First you need a large pot, I mean a pot big enough to sit in, get the picture? A big pot.

Now, chop up six garlic cloves and four onions.

Have a stubbie.

This is to feed four people – with leftovers for the dog, if you want your dog to smell like a gamey Italian waiter. If someone turns up uninvited at tea time they can sit and watch the dog eat his. Ha ha ha.

Chop up some peppers, capsicums, tomatoes, carrots and potatoes – in fact any veggie that comes to hand.

Have a stubbie.

If it moves, kill it and cut it up. If it grows, pull it out and chop it up. This is the general thinking. Put a great whack of butter in the pot and turn up the heat. Toss your garlic and onions in with a table spoon of Keens Curry Powder.

Have a stubbie.

Let that fry away lightly for a while then toss in all your veggies, then rip open a can – a large can of Heinz Beef Broth barley and veggies, and toss that in. Add water.

Have a stubbie.

Add Kikhoman Soy Sauce and a hearty whack of old El Paso Thick 'n' Chunky Salsa.

Have a piss (not in the pot) to make space to add another stubbie, to taste.

More heat, then you add your sliced meat, lamb or beef all chopped up in to bite-size bits. One spoon of cornflour, chopped up. Mushrooms can be added, and a spoon of hot mustard. Personally, I like to add chopped liver and kidney to this. Animal ones if you can get them.

Then, when you have it on the boil, add your macaroni or pasta for the posh among you reading this, and that's Chopper's Hot Pot.

Now you got to give this a bit of time to stew and sort of cook away. For the herb lovers a handful of mixed herbs can be tossed out the window, but nowhere near my Hot Pot.

If it doesn't look thick enough add more veggies, chopped celery and spring onions, but I'm betting it will come up a treat. I like to add a dash of milk to my Hot Pot.

Once ready it is served with ice-cold beer. Always leave cans of beer in freezer for three minutes before serving. *Bon Appetito*.

I CAME home drunk and bit the dog on the ear. My wife told me if I ever bit Little Bill again she would axe me to death in my sleep. I think she is serious. I was just talking to the dog in a language he would understand. Needless to say a domestic had erupted. I have a hot pot on the stove, and am being told that if I bite the dog again I'm a dead man. Am I to take any of this seriously? While cooking the hot pot and having a beer to wash down the taste of dog's ear out of my mouth I let my mind wander.

I've always got two sets of phone numbers to ring in case I visit Melbourne or Sydney and both sets of numbers will deliver and suck it till its unblocked and even bring a dozen cans and a pizza with 'em.

One set are female media types and the other charge $200 per hour. Frank Sinatra was right. You can call him all the names you like but he was right, believe me.

CHAPTER 14

THE SEWER I LEFT

'For those who think they got away with it because Dennis and Helga are dead, I have bad news. Polaroids were taken.'

HIS name was Terry Flannery. He was a dead-set junkie crim, a nitwit, tough-guy dwarf. His only saving grace was his girlfriend, Helga. Helga was the classic big blonde prostitute. She was the sort of chick everyone had screwed but no one admitted to it.

Helga could screw a bloke for a year and not know his last name and not even bother asking. She was a big-picture girl who didn't let her mind get cluttered with detail.

She kept every boyfriend she ever had alive and fully funded. She was a workhorse and would work seven nights a week in parlours in and around inner-city Melbourne. Flexi-legs, but no flexi-time.

She would work full of speed meth-amphetamine and relax on heroin, then she worked on heroin and relaxed on speed.

Hey, Helga, do us a favour, will you? She would get into your car and blow you and your mates for free as long as it built credit. The chick's life ran on credit. She needed men to owe her a favour and a lot of those favours got repaid. She could run up drug bills worth thousands and pay them off with her arse.

The dealer and his mates owned her. She was owned by dozens of dealers, but the biggest was Mister Death, Dennis Bruce Allen. The stories of Helga sucking guys off in Allen's house in Cubitt Street, Richmond, while Dennis shot them in the head are famous.

They got a head job, all right, but not the one they planned. Dennis would get Helga to signal him, he'd watch the guy's face and eyes and Helga would wave a hand as the bloke blew and as she swallowed Dennis would pull the trigger. Dennis would masturbate as he watched, with his gun in the other hand, then fire the fatal shots. Then Helga would crawl over and polish Dennis off with a head job.

She would get a few grams of heroin for this and a shower before being kicked out of 49 Cubitt Street. Dennis was a sick bastard.

He would get desperate junkies to perform sex acts with dogs as a way of repaying debts. He had fourteen-year-old prostitutes and their thirty-two-year-old mothers put on lesbian acts or get sisters to screw brothers.

Heroin was the master, Dennis was the ringmaster and all else simply part of his circus. They reckon it was Helga Wagnegg who was actually screwing Victor Gouroff on the lounge suite when Dennis axed him to death. Now that's a real chop-up.

The truth of this I don't know, but Helga was a bitch on heat. She loved drugs and she loved sex and admitted that she was a slut with no place left to go but down and few if any had been down as low as Helga.

She would put on sex parties and have sex with policemen friendly to Dennis. And for those who think they may have got away with it because both Dennis and Helga are no longer with us, I have bad news. Polaroid photos would be taken and they are still about. Dennis would laugh out loud at the Cherry Tree Hotel, and no wonder.

Helga had her nice side now and again. When no one was looking she would give you a smile if she liked you, just a warm, friendly, little-girl smile. It was just a moment of recognition from one human to another.

I got a few of Helga's smiles and I smiled and nodded back then she would return to the living valley of death she called life.

Helga was once a top-looking lady, all tits and legs. She could have been a movie star or at least a porno queen. She wasn't ugly, she just became ugly and she knew that the men she loved so much would one day be the death of her.

She seemed to love the company of men she knew would bash her near to death or kill her if she did not obey them or if she crossed them. In the end she got her wish.

It was felt Helga had turned dog and was going to give evidence against Dennis and other members of the crew and that was her death warrant.

She was killed and dumped in the Yarra. Even had she lived to give evidence, who could a junkie hooker hurt in court?

She was basically killed because she ended up disgusting even men like Allen. She was a living reminder of what scum they had all become and she had to go. She had to be blotted from their minds.

However, as one man who had smiled at Helga and caused her to smile back, I can only recall the little girl's face and for a moment the innocence within all evil shone out at me and hit me like sunshine.

Dennis Allen was maybe one of the most evil monsters in Melbourne criminal history. I nearly killed the bloke in 1975 in B Division, Pentridge, and I deeply regret my moment of Christian kindness. If I had killed him, I wonder how many people would be alive today. Would Helga? Probably not, she was always committing suicide in instalments with the needle as her preferred weapon.

But as I flutter through the pages of my memory I can recall Dennis as a happy, fun-loving, cheeky young scallywag who would rather do you a good turn then a bad one and I wonder at the monster that took Dennis by the hand and walked him into the valley. Dennis did not wish to be the best of the best, he wanted to be the master of all evil and madness and he almost got there. He wasn't the worst but my oath he came close. The only thing he didn't do was eat human flesh and I've got no evidence that he never did that either.

Wayne Stanhope, Greg Pasche, Vic Gouroff, Anton Kenny and 'The Hairdresser'. I don't know his name, but he got shot for giving Dennis a bad hair cut.

I pity none of them. Call me soft hearted but I sort of feel a bit sorry for Helga. She may have had a sick and evil heart but she also had a big heart and for a kind word and a smile she would walk over broken glass for you. A kind word and a pat on the head ... she was like an animal in that regard.

That's all she ever really wanted, but in the end she got a bucket of water poured down her neck and a heroin needle up her arm, gang banged in the arse and tossed in the Yarra. The valley of the shadow of death, few if any walk through it. Poor Helga, here's a smile for you, Princess. Rest in peace. Whatever you deserved, you didn't deserve that.

Am I getting sentimental and soft hearted in my old age?

I LOOK back on the past and friends and foes alike with a fond sentiment and sadness as we all walked through that same valley. Even old coppers like Rocket Rod Porter, Dirty Larry Curnow, Barry the Boy Hahnel, Garry Schipper, the late John Hill but to name a small, small few.

All coppers who had a hand in creation of the myth that became the monster. Whether they knew it or not my friends and my enemies have all helped to create the myth of Chopper Read, a myth based on reality but a reality that was so insane it was in fact partly fiction. Am I making sense?

If one examines the life of Dennis Bruce Allen one can only wonder if it all really happened. I know Peter Allen quite well and of all that clan Peter was the thinker – as cold blooded as all the rest put together but a thinker. Yet, for all his mad insanity he never lost his soul. He never lost the ability to laugh at his own life.

In other words, he never took himself too seriously. I think therein lies the secret key to walking through the shadow of the valley and coming out alive.

A sense of comedy, the ability to laugh at yourself and your own situation and when you come out the other end you look back and wonder what it was all about. The crims and the coppers that wade through the sewer of blood, guts and drugs can only come out the other side half sane if they keep a sense of humour. If they ever acknowledged that it is all real and not some cops and robbers game they would go mad.

The friends and enemies alike you began with are for the most part all dead and you're surrounded by a new world you don't understand. Full of new people who don't understand you.

But I sit in my chicken shed and look out across the farm and I notice that the land hasn't changed: the sky, the trees, the grass, the smoke coming from the kitchen chimney. Banjo Paterson could be sitting next to me and out here on the land he'd hardly know it from a hundred years ago.

It is hard to believe that all that has happened to me and all that I have done to others really happened. I scratch where my ears used to be and feel the hole in my head where the ice pick went in and I know it was real.

It must have happened for there to be a Chopper Read. There must have been a life for him to lead and as I clean my glasses to put them back on my fat eighteen-stone face I squint at the morning sun and wonder in puzzlement at the myth that is my own life ... but not for long.

Fact is, she who walks on water has arisen, and I must down pen and attend to the septic tank. I've gone from court bail to bailing the dunny. It's a shit of a job but it's better than being in jail, that's for sure.

I HAVE a friend in America named Sam Risovich, from Sparks County, Nevada. I have kept in touch with him for some time. Big Sam Risovich sends me books on the Wild West and the old gun fighters, a great love of mine. Then he sent me a book called *The Official Guide to the Best Cat Houses in Nevada.*

An Italian friend of mine was visiting Las Vegas, Nevada. His name is Charlie Monza and I insisted he visit the famed Mustang Ranch just east of Reno Nevada, Storey County. Charlie said he knew the guy who owns it or used to, a bloke called Joe Conforte.

The Mustang Ranch is eight and a bit miles from the Reno Nevada Hilton Hotel. You take interstate eighty east to the Mustang off-ramp exit twenty-three miles, drive straight ahead about a mile, just past the auto wreckers on your right and follow the road under the railroad tracks and the Mustang Ranch will be right in front of you. The most famous whore house in America and guess what?

There is a lady there named Ingrid and another named Cherry who have read every single one of my books. I always said hookers have top tastes in matters of culture. Evidently my books and my two CDs are collectors items in certain areas of America such as whore houses and state and federal prisons, not to mention a few Sheriffs' Departments and the odd mental home.

If they knew that the boy in the book had become an alcoholic chicken farmer who looks more like Colonel Sanders than Hannibal Lecter they would be shattered. But to Sam Risovich and family I say thanks for the friendship and remember, don't believe everything you read unless the author has an extensive criminal record. Ha, ha.

CHARLIE Monza is a tough little Sicilian. *La Casa de la Monza*. We have been friends since our school days and if I have to be pushed into it, I guess I'd have to say Charlie is what the movies would call a made man. He lives in Punta Raisi, a suburb of Palermo, Sicily. Punta Raisi is where the Palermo airport is.

It's not the posh end of town – if Palermo has a posh end, that is. But the Monza crew openly control the airport. It's an open secret. The kid from Thomastown ended up becoming a real-life Robert de Niro. What Alphonse pretended to be, Charlie Monza and Tommy Caprice, both former Thomastown boys, are in real life.

They are now both so high up in their own world they are the dreams men like Alphonse have when they are under the blanket having a fiddle.

What goons like Alphonse could never grasp was that it was never about money – neither Charlie or Tommy would own more than two pair of shoes each. One for day wear, one pair for church, weddings and funerals. And these guys are in their own quiet, polite, modest manner the men Hollywood make such a fuss of. We exchange postcards and letters and the odd phone call. Their business is their business. They think my books are high comedy and they would know.

Oops, speaking of business, the man coming to put the new wood heater in the top room wants to use the toilet and I haven't unblocked the septic tank. Back soon.

Now if you want your train of thought to be upset, unblock a septic pipe with your bare hands. The critics always said I was full of shit and maybe they were right all along.

Where was I? Yes, Charlie and Tommy, the only two people on earth who loved my crime-fiction books and thought my real-life books a bit of a yawn. You can't please everyone. Oh well.

We now have a second wood heater installed and the washing machine blew up. Life on the farm is a stagger from one broken thing to the next. The septic tank has been emptied by hand and bucket.

I'm going up the pub. I don't know about your temper but mine is slightly frayed at the edges. The washing-machine man has now arrived. I still haven't got to the pub.

For an alcoholic with a history of criminal insanity this is most upsetting but I cannot leave until he goes. To think that a man once considered one of the most dangerous criminals in Australian history must now wait for the washing-machine repair man.

Ned Kelly would turn in his grave. The whole thing is quite Monty Python. I don't believe any of this is really happening. Barman, where are you when I need you?

I'VE just returned from the pub (burp). A quick dozen ten-ounce beers does wonders for the human condition.

Did I tell you that old Doug Young sold the Richmond Arms Hotel to Damien Waller and John Young, both sons of policemen? Damien is the stepson of Assistant Commissioner Barry Bennett. Damien and John hired me as the bouncer.

I mean the whole pub was run by coppers, owned by coppers, Barry Bennett's young son, Ty Bennett, himself a policeman, lived above the pub.

Off-duty cops drank in the place. The whole pub was wall to wall police and they hired me as the bouncer.

When they called last orders I asked young Ty Bennett and his friends to leave, not knowing the bloke lived in the pub. I was patrolling the car park and a well-known local lass was bent over the bonnet of a HQ Holden getting some close attention in the pants department from an off-duty policeman.

She was getting frisked – the hard way. If that's the way they do a search these days I'm glad I've turned honest.

I saw the lady's husband inside and, when questioned, told him she was being ill in the lady's toilet. He accepted this, not asking me how the hell I'd know.

Young Ty died in a car crash while on duty not long after, may he rest in peace. He wasn't a bad kid, full of laughs and life and fun and not a snob. Policemen who walk up to me and say hello and have a drink are made up of two sorts: the old hard heads and the young carefrees. One lot have the rank, the other lot don't care. It's the ladder climbers who become snobby. Both young Ty and his old dad Barry Bennett are (were in Ty Bennett's case, sadly) cut from the same cloth. They reckon only the good die young. That was true in Ty Bennett's case. A nice young bloke and a good style of a copper.

On the second night I acted as bouncer at the Richmond Arms I was going to belt some wombat and young Ty stepped in and pulled the young mug up, saved me and the other bloke a bit of trouble.

I didn't bounce at the pub after that. If a normal bouncer hits someone, big deal. If I do it, big trouble. You get a strange feeling when a bloke you know dies, even if you have only known the chap for a few drinks and a few hellos over a few nights. The here today, gone tomorrow thing hits you.

I've waved some good friends and bad enemies goodbye and death sort of blankets you in a wave of strange sentiment. It's hard to explain. You might think that for someone like me it would be easy but it gets harder. Outside of war, I would think I have seen more friends and enemies die than anyone in Australia. I feel that, although I have left the world of violence death will be near me forever. I didn't know Ty at all well but he was a good bloke. Anyway, young Ty, this one's for you, *via con dios, amigo*.

IT is lamb-marking season. We have to clip the lambs' ears and ring their tails and nut the young males – where's Nick the Greek when you need him? Let me tell you there is no Silence of the Lambs out here. They bleat like buggery after the 'operation' until they get a drink from their mums to calm them down, and you can't blame them.

Poppy season is on us again, too. Opium poppies, peas, barley, oats, wheat, the lot. The poppies are a funny crop – $1,650 a ton from the factory, that's what the farmer gets. Or you can gamble on the juice content being higher and get $2,000 a ton – or $200 if its lower – but the factory will gamble and pay a straight-out $1,650 a ton.

The young kids and would-be crooks who rob the poppy fields are a smart lot. I was walking home late one night on one of my few rare nights out and caught or saw three teenagers standing in the pea paddock. The peas were in full flower, and they were pulling the peas out and stuffing them into bags.

The paddock on the other side of the road had the poppies in flower but some local had wisely hung a 'strictly prohibited area' sign on the pea field. The three kids ran off with their garbage bag full of peas on seeing me. Even now, would-be drug dealers run when they see The

Chopper. Could you imagine those clowns? They would boil up their bounty and then expect to get high. It would give them as much of a buzz as smoking sweetcorn. Anyway, the poppies are only any good if you have a multi-million dollar processing factory and unless you're willing to rob a harvester and a truck full of poppies and hijack the factory you're kidding yourself.

There are ways and means and the right time of the year and so forth and so on but a lot of kids have killed themselves in the foolish attempt to become drug kings by boiling up poppies and playing with the leftovers.

I mean, if everyone could become a millionaire overnight by pinching a bag of green poppies in flower there would be a hell of a lot of rich bastards in Tassie.

Nothing is as it appears. The poppy police are there more to stop idiots killing themselves than anything else. The deadly wives' tales relating to the back-yard processing of the poppy plant are legend and, by the way, the farmer makes more dough out of a good pea year than an average poppy year.

It's like sheep. It would be cheaper to shoot 'em then shear 'em. Anyone who has spent a day in the hot sun dipping sheep would agree. I would shoot the dumb bastards just for pleasure. The day of the small farmer with 250 to 300 head is over.

My father-in-law ran a few thousand sheep when wool was a pound a pound but these days it's all crops. My father-in-law, old E.V. Hodge, reckons that they are turning us all into vegetable growers. Aussie land don't ride on the sheep's back no more. Buggered if I know whose back we are riding on, but he's not going bah bah, that's for sure.

Sheep are more a meat market now. The wool is a pest sideline. My father-in-law tells a story about an outraged shearer who showed him the local newspaper. It read MAN AND SHEARER DIE IN CAR CRASH. The shearer was complaining that the newspaper didn't even consider a shearer to be part of the human race. I've spent a few days in a shearing shed and that's why I'd rather shoot 'em than shear 'em. The sheep, that is. Not the poor bloody shearers. The old Banjo Paterson romantic notion of the shearer is a load of crap as well. Bloody hard work for no thanks and even less money if you ask me, and sheep are the most stupid animals God ever shovelled guts into.

The farmer was once the backbone of the nation, or so the story went. Some of them are precious, delicate, whinging old pansies from what I've seen so far, although there are always exceptions and contradictions to every rule.

I've met some good strong hard and true men on the land. As for the rest I'd plough the bastards in and bury them under the bloody land.

The gossiping, back stabbing, pack of old girls, they can dish it out but they can't take it. The man on the land is a great comic with a sense of fun and hi jinx that so delighted men like Banjo Paterson as long as it was on their terms. It's still out there in the bush and alive today but when the laugh turns in their direction they don't like it, let me tell you.

I'm afraid I hold a more Lawson type view of the land and the men on it. In the words of my father-in-law, let it be known if you have a Chubb safe, then hide your money elsewhere. Remember, no one in the bush can keep a secret, and if your sheep is eating someone else's grass then it's someone else's sheep.

IF it rains the farmer will say we could do with a bit of sun, if the sun shines, we could do with a bit of rain, if there is no wind he wants wind, if it's a windy day he will complain, and every year is a bad year.

The poor farmer is always broke. The cost of keeping his wife's Jaguar on the road is killing him. As he scrapes the mud off his boot on entering the bank the old farmer is a sad sight indeed.

But while the city yuppies stand in line to see the teller, the farmer is allowed to moan his troubles to the manager.

Mateship in the bush? The word mateship was forged before and during World War I. Of course all country towns have their war monuments but ninety per cent of all men who went to the First and Second World War came from the dusty, dirty cities because farming came under the heading of a reserved occupation, as did waterside workers, another stalwart, courageous breed of Australian who believe they carry the nation on their backs just like the sheep.

You know who went to war. The Aussie battler, the unemployed, the farm worker, the factory worker, shopkeeper, street sweeper, ditch digger, shit carter, the butcher, the baker and the candlestick maker, wood choppers and rock breakers. Every bastard Banjo Paterson forgot to write about. You see, Banjo came from the landed gentry so naturally his view on Australia and the Australian was seen through the eyes of a gent who never did a real day's manual work in his life. It hurts me to say so, but he was a self-confessed lawyer, and we all know about them. (See above.)

I'm starting to sound like a Communist. I'm sorry. I was on about mateship. If you check your nation's prisons you'll find city boys doing life sentences and manslaughter sentences for coming to the aid of a mate with a broken bottle, iron bar, or baseball bat.

You won't find many country lads doing time for backing up their mates. Now there are contradictions and exceptions to every rule, but as a general thing, if you get in a fight in a country pub then, mate, you're on your fucking own. If you win they will talk about you afterwards – and if you lose they'll leave you in the gutter to be eaten by the foxes. I've never been left posted in a fight in Collingwood, meaning my mates didn't run and leave me, but I've seen some poor bastards get kicked near to death and left for dead and not a mate to help them in country pubs.

You can be the loneliest bloke in the world lying on the floor of a country pub while about six bronzed Aussies sink the slipper. The rest will sit and watch as though it's a bad play.

Then the buggers make a liar out of me. During a bush fire everyone pitches in without being asked. I think the bush fire or fire in general is a common human enemy and that might be the contradiction.

Anyway, as you can see, I don't view the bush or the people in it with any Banjo Paterson style romantic nonsense. People who get misty-eyed about the bush usually live in cities, wear their Blundstone boots to go shopping and the closest they get to stock is when the check their share portfolio.

Good blokes are good blokes be they in the bush or in the city and a maggot is a maggot wherever you find him and the bush is no exception. However, when it's all said and done, where would I rather live? The bush or the city? The bush, of course. The snakes are just as deadly but they move a little slower.

FOR cops and robbers, it's a haunted world. Every cop and every gangster walks with the ghosts of the men who went before them, reminding them all that there was always someone bigger and better before they ever came along.

I was determined to defy my ghosts and go far beyond the normal and the extraordinary and even superhuman. I was determined to become the biggest, most insanely feared criminal identity in Melbourne. I had a sense of history, I knew what the hard men before me did so I did what they all did and more; removing my ears at the age of twenty-four was my simple way of welcoming the Melbourne police, prison and criminal world to my nightmare and it was a nightmare none of them was ready for.

I introduced a level of violence, torture, murder and sheer fear unheard of before. I took it to the limit, then beyond. I entered the shadow of the valley and for nearly twenty five years I was in that world and the valley became a darker place.

I shouldn't really count my few years in the Tasmanian prison system and criminal world because that is like comparing a Barbie doll with a rattlesnake. But from late 1969 to 1991 Melbourne was my valley and no one stood in my way. A large boast but a true one.

Kill me or cop it sweet, that's the way I saw it. In or out of prison no one could take more pain than me, no one could dish out more pain than me. I wasn't about to stand in the shadow of any man who went before me.

Every crim in Melbourne stood in the shadow of Ned Kelly and Squizzy Taylor, Jackie Twist, Normie Bradshaw, Billy 'The Texan' Longley, Jimmy 'The Pom' Driscoll, the Kane brothers, Ray Chuck, Freddie 'The Frog' Harrison'. I said fuck 'em all.

I said as a kid that one day when they write the criminal history of the nation there will be only three names, Ned Kelly, Squizzy Taylor and Chopper Read and all the rest can buy a ticket and watch the fucking movie although I don't think Mick Jagger would play me, do you?

I mean, I ran on an insanity level never before seen and I doubt will be repeated, and the fact that I came out of it alive to end up a fat-arsed chicken farmer with glasses, a local piss pot in a local town is, in my opinion, the most insane part of my whole insane story. It also helps that hanging was pretty well abolished by the time I got stuck into it. I might have ended up having a hearty last meal in the condemned cell if I'd been born a century ago. They were still necking crooks in the

1920s and 1930s. But I lived to tell the tale, as a writer of books and the spinner of yarns. Why, oh why didn't I end up dead? And they say there isn't a God. Well, if there isn't, then I'm the luckiest bastard alive.

After a run in with Graeme Jensen in Bendigo prison he told me later I was either the maddest bastard he had ever heard of or I had more guts than God. I think guts was the word. I don't really believe I was ever mad, I prefer to think – in my saner moments, at least – that I was just a straight-out tough bastard with a twisted sense of humour.

The criminal world is an ego-driven place but it is also full of piss-weak bastards. I mean physically the biggest crims in Australian history before me and Neddy Smith and Ned Kelly were basically little better then dwarfs, pipsqueaks and runts, not physically strong men. Drugs haven't made them any bigger or stronger, just more treacherous. Big, strong, healthy bastards really stand out in the criminal world. Your average crook is 5 feet 7 inches tall and 11 or 12 stone and that's saying something.

Big physical crims really stand out and physically big strong crims who are as nutty as fruit cakes and carry guns – well, they are few and far between and demand some respect. Had I taken up football I'd be Mr Average, but I was bound for glory in the criminal world. Lets face it, how could I lose? Ned Kelly was a horse thief who wore a bucket on his head and Squizzy Taylor was a dwarf with a gun in his hand. Let's face it, you don't have to try too hard to earn a criminal reputation but you do have to get to the other end alive to tell the story and that part, I admit, is tricky. I was a shooting (literally) star who didn't quite burn out. I don't know why. I would like to think it was because I was so tough and smart but the truth is, in the end, it was luck.

If Bluey Brazel had stuck that knife in one inch to the left I was dead back during the overcoat war in Pentridge, and no books would be written and I'd be just another crazy dead crim.

People think most crims want to keep in the shadows but many of them are ego driven and love the headlines and publicity. They don't know that the biggest headlines they will ever make is when they are lying in a pool of their own blood, shot dead by an unknown gunman as they walk home.

They finally make the big time but they are lying on the slab in the morgue at the time. I got out alive – God knows how. Tricky, indeed.

POSTSCRIPT: The truth is that 99.9 per cent of the physically big men who enter the criminal world aren't worth a you know what full of cold water. (What a silly expression, a you know what full of water would be warm, wouldn't it?)

So I guess you could say big crims with any guts, heart and dash are freaks in that respect. If that is true, then I was a freak.

Many of the big men who try to be standover men only become targets for the police, press and other crims. He is a good scalp to have. A small man with a gun hiding in the bushes beats some giant who can bench press three hundred pounds. Rat cunning and mental strength beats boneheaded strength. A lion may have the roar but is no match for a mouse with a magnum. Or, as one of my publishers says his grandfather told him, 'It wasn't Abraham Lincoln who made all men equal, son. It was Samuel Colt.'

AS with old football players, boxers and sportsmen, in any physical high-risk area there comes a time to walk away. The ones who end up dead are mostly men who over-stayed their time. When the barman yells last orders you leave, and I left.

Had I stayed on I would have become more a figure of comedy than a figure of fear. There is nothing more embarrassing in my opinion than some over-the-hill old fart who still thinks he's a tough guy. I honestly don't think that would have happened as I would never have lived long enough to reach the point of being an object of embarrassment.

I was always quicker and smarter than the snakes I hunted and once I slowed down the odds were against me, and in my (old) business you never punt against the odds. You don't see many old mongooses, do you? Or as they used to say about fighter pilots in wartime: there are old pilots and there are bold pilots, but there are no old, bold pilots.

If I had kept going I would have had to become more violent to make up for my age. I would not have been able to bash or stab or give people a light touch of the blue flame. I would have had to shoot every enemy through the head.

I would have had to recruit young turks (or more likely Albanians) to be the muscle I once was. I would have had to become the coach rather than the star player. Better to get out while at the top, or maybe at the bottom.

I guess if I'm honest the books saved me and I will always owe my publishers a debt of gratitude. I was lucky to find two money-hungry spivs who saw the chance to profit from my pain. At least they didn't rip me off but they weren't lawyers, after all.

My ego tells me that had I not written one about myself some other prick would have so it's only fair I got the money.

Nevertheless to Sly and Greedy, thank you. And in the immortal words of Brian Kane when he learnt that his young nephew was having ballet lessons, 'I wonder where I'd be today if I had have taken up ballet dancing.' The girls would have loved Brian in *Swan Lake* when he had a magnum stuffed down the front of his leotard. The problem might be when he shot some socialite in the front row when he did his first squat in the first Act. In other words only God or the Devil knows where I'd be today had I not met up with Sly and Greedy. I no longer carry a gun. It mightn't seem much to you, but for me not to carry a gun was a huge decision. I felt naked walking around without a shooter. But for me to carry a gun meant that eventually I would use it. It would be like a smoker carrying a pack of fags when he's trying to give up.

Now don't get me wrong, I'm no born-again pacifist. I'd be lying if I tried to tell you I didn't know where to get my hands on a gun in a hurry in case the Indians attack and we have to circle the wagons, but I no longer carry a gun and I no longer break the law.

I swore never to have children because a crook with kids can be got at through his children. I knew if I ever did have a child my life would have to change. And so it has.

I'm soon to be a father and like all fathers I don't want my son to have my life, that's fair enough. A dad wanting a better life for his son than he had himself. I'm not part of some criminal dynasty, nor do I wish to start one. I'm a freak, I was never meant to be but I was and now I am no more and I wouldn't wish what I went through on anyone – least of all, my own son.

I have gone all philosophical so here is another message for you. Never build a chicken shed when you're pissed.

MY spelling is often called into question, a matter I find most offensive so I will relate one of the rare stories I have been told by my wife. She who walks on water told me of an Irish policeman who came across a bombing with bits of human bodies all over the place. He pulled out his pen and paper and began to take notes. He saw one hand lying on the road. 'How do you spell road?' he said to himself and wrote down 'Roed'. Then he found a leg and a foot on the road and wrote down leg and foot on 'Roed'. Then he came across a hand in the gutter. 'How do you spell gutter?' he thought, then wrote down hand found in 'Guta'. Then he found a human head on the footpath. The Irish policeman thought, 'footpath, footpath, how do I spell that?' Then, looking about quickly, he kicked the head on to the road. Then, smiling, he wrote that a human head was found on the 'Roed'.

I know how he feels.

My father-in-law, Ernie Hodge, tells a yarn about two old farmers who walked past each other every morning. 'Morning,' one would say. 'Morning,' the other would reply, and for twenty-odd years these were the only words spoken between the two. 'Morning,' one would say and 'morning,' the other would reply. Then one morning one farmer spoke.

'My horse is sick,' he said.

'Morning,' replied the other.

'Morning,' said the farmer with the sick horse, and walked on.

The following day they approached each other again.

'When my horse was sick I gave him paraffin and molasses,' said the second farmer, then said, 'morning,' and walked by.

'Morning,' said the other.

The next day the two farmers approached again.

'I gave my horse paraffin and molasses and he died,' said the farmer with the sick horse.

'So did mine,' replied the other.

And I thought the jokes in jail were bad.

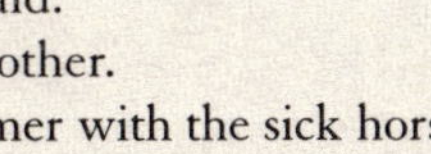

CHAPTER 15

A ROLE MODEL FOR DRUNKS

'These bikie gangs always have hangers-on prepared to kill to get their full colours, so there are always plenty of soldiers prepared to die ...'

WHEN I got out I ended up knocking around with a few tearaways and there were photos taken of me with what appeared to be guns. I was charged with a few minor offences after the photos were mysteriously circulated around.

So it was back to Michael Hodgeman's office and back into my wallet to pay him. It was then the truth came out: the guns were obviously replicas (pull the other one – Ed.) and the charges were dropped.

It was an expensive but important lesson for me. If the police were so insanely desperate to lock me up, what would they do if they caught me really doing the wrong thing.

It was the sharp lesson I needed. If it had not happened I am sure I would have drifted back to the old ways and would be back in jail now. It was a reminder that the police took me more seriously than I took myself.

When I got out back in 1991 I was determined to keep out of jail but when I got to Tassie I drifted back into bad company and I ended up back inside.

I usually only last about six months out. The cops would give me enough rope to hang myself, but this time they moved too soon. It was the wake-up call I needed and if I'd had any guns – which, of course, I didn't – they were dumped.

It was time to make the break.

Finally.

For good.

Forever.

But I will never end my quest to get a firearms licence back. I have been involved in a tongue-in-cheek battle with the authorities to get a rotten .22 bolt action or a shotgun like any other farmer.

I believe they will never change and I think they believe that writing to me saying I cannot have a gun is the same as writing to a monkey, saying don't eat peanuts.

I am a law-abiding citizen and as a farmer you need a firearm to protect yourself from snakes, the slithering types and the two-legged ones.

I NOTICE from my country retreat that the bikies have been at it again. You would have seen reports that the big international bikie gangs had a meeting in Sydney and decided there was room for about six main gangs in Australia.

The little gangs were given a choice, join us or get flogged. For most it wasn't a hard choice. In the end the knifings, bombings, shootings and all that shit have nothing to do with honour or turf or any of that bullshit.

It is the biggest drug war there has ever been in Australia. This is the battle for the control of the meth-amphetamines market. People can die for as little as $100, so could you imagine what people will do for the billion-dollar industry.

These bikie gangs always have hangers-on prepared to kill to get their full colours, so there are always plenty of soldiers prepared to die so they can curry favour from the generals.

They are like the Mafia except they wear leather instead of silk suits. The bikie leaders know that if they don't get control there will be chaos. The biggest speed king, Johnny Higgs, has been locked up so there is a big market to fill.

The people pulling the strings are the American bikie gangs who have passed their instructions over to their local little brothers.

In 1995 the police grabbed the world's largest amphetamines lab worth $488 million, including $24 million in pure speed. Now this was in Australia: are you starting to get the picture? People will bash their grans for the price of a hit so what would they do for an empire of speed? In America the bikies and the Italians have become very close and the same thing has happened in Australia.

Behind every gang of bikies you'll find the Italians controlling the product. After all, bikies aren't fucking Avon ladies and someone has to sell it.

Mad Charlie controlled the chemicals for the manufacture of methamphetamines in Australia. He did business with Italians and bikies and some of the bikies even crewed up with the Asian triads in the heroin trade. They would do this on the quiet because heroin is supposed to be a no no in the bikie world.

Mad Charlie had the personal home numbers of most of the main bosses of the American clubs, including the one-time boss of the Fort Lauderdale Outlaws Gang, Clarence Smith, who was convicted of five murders in 1997. He executed four bikies and then bombed a witness in New Orleans. He had the number of the most powerful member of the American Hells Angels, a man he called 'Sonny'.

Basically Charlie told me that by the year 2000 it would be all organised crime and he said that by then the funny thing would be they would all be working for us. Now I didn't think for a moment he meant Tasmanian chicken farmers and by the way he jokingly pushed his nose in the air I knew he meant the Italians.

'You don't think Old Pauly and Popa Tony and Eddie C are just gonna sit back and watch some blokes who think they are in the remake of *Easy Rider* just cruise into town and take over the game? They need the chemicals and they need the docks so they need us. They need a distribution network so they need us even more. They can get the headlines and we can get the money. It seems fair to me.'

He said that the Hells Angels were the gang that was in control but he didn't care who came out on top. It'll be the gang with the most guns and the biggest pull in America, but basically they may be gang members but they aren't gangsters. They are squareheads who ride bikes with a nose full of speed and arms covered in tattoos.

'They are easy to control. Personally, I am more worried about the Chinese,' said Charlie.

It doesn't matter about all the bombings and the deaths because the bikies still have to go to men named Dominic, Angelo, Nino, Carmine,

Bruno, Rocco and Tony to get the chemicals. You control the chemicals and you control the product.

There is a small group of men who have multi-millions invested in the illegal drug industry and none of them ride motorbikes and they won't be giving up control just because of some so-called 2000 agreement. Remember where you read it first.

A HAND from the past reached out and tapped me on the shoulder not long ago and I made a phone call I thought I'd never have to make again to a lifelong brother and friend I had turned my back on in the name of domestic and family normality.

Dave the Jew was glad to hear from me and he jested that if Mad Charlie had shot him (Dave the Jew) in Dave's front yard then my son would now be called Dave and not Charlie.

Please do not read too much into such a comic remark, as who shot Mad Charlie is the business of the man who did it and the one who gave the order, and the price of a book doesn't warrant the keys to the Kingdom of Knowledge. No offence, I hope. You only get that sort of inside information from a $50 hardback. Only joking.

I explained to The Jew the concern my wife and I had regarding a certain person wishing to visit me, and that this person had contacted both my father and father-in-law. Dave gave his little giggle and told me the problem vanished the moment I rang him.

'Forget about it, mate, he will never make the airport.'

The phone call was the sad contradiction of my life. I want to bury Chopper Read so that the chicken farmer can replace the gangster.

I am a once was, has been and glad of it. But when my peace and quiet is threatened I still reserve the right to ring up a man who the professional hitmen of Australia look upon as their hero.

It is strange to talk to a man who can smile and say 'don't worry' and you know that means that someone is about to die.

He is the perfect hitman because he has no criminal record to speak of and so the police of the nation view him as they would a fairy story. But in the criminal world, his name is worth its weight in coffins.

The fact that he is regarded as a believe-it-or-not suits Dave. Unlike Mad Charlie, Dave did not seek the headlines and the reputation, his name was made in blood. Other people's. Our phone call ended with

The Jew, almost tearfully, agreeing to be little Charlie's Godfather. I don't want my son to follow in my footsteps but I don't want no one kicking sand in his face when he goes to the beach, either.

It's like the Jewish Muslim who went to the Pope for confession. 'What are you doing here?' asked the Pope.

'Just having a bet each way,' said the Jewish Muslim.

I don't want little Charlie falling under the influence of the wrong type of person so why not have the most dangerous man in the country in the shadows just to make sure?

CHAPTER 16

THEM OLD PUB BLUES

'I change to Crown Lagers ... their thin necks make them excellent to use in a serious pub brawl.'

THERE is a unique psychological point of interest I'd like to make. I haven't been in a fight in or outside a pub since 1987. Well, I did have to smack a few wombats to the ground in those days but that was just a little workout in the name of good humour rather than a serious desire to maim anyone.

Then I was young and silly and in my thirties, now I am forty-five and the days of pub brawling are behind me.

When I walk into a pub now I see the look on the face of a smart-arse sometimes, a would-be punch-on artist who would like to get a reputation. The look says: 'He doesn't look that tough to me and I reckon I could take him.' I will then look at him and give a little smile and wink and I can see their tiny minds ticking over: 'What if he's carrying a gun or a weapon? No, he's only wearing a T-shirt. He's got a bull neck, big arms and big shoulders but he's gone too fat. He'll run out of puff. He may be strong but he is no longer fast. I'll wait until he gets a bit more pissed.' While these numbnuts are going through these mental equations they should notice that I will change to drinking Crown Lagers, not because I am a toff, but because their thin necks make them excellent to use in a serious pub brawl. Grab the neck and smash the bottom and you could rip the neck out of King Kong. The art of using a Crown Lager, beer glass or pool cue in a pub brawl seems to be lost on the youth of today. They pull a syringe from their puny arms and wave it around and expect to get respect.

The point is that some of these so-called tough guys could easily punch the shit out of me, but even the dimmest must know there's always tomorrow. 'I don't want my house burnt down or a hole put in my back one dark night,' is what they should be thinking.

I look over and I can see them relax. 'Fuck it, he isn't bothering me, why should I bother him?' Good idea.

I always recall the words of the great Ronnie Kray: 'No one beats a legend.' But as The Texan once said, anyone who drinks in a pub can be got at.

This is no longer a great issue to me as a new father, a chicken farmer and wood cutter. I will slip out every now and again for a quiet one but no longer get physical. If I get on the tear eventually there will be some punk who wants a go and if I win I will end up in jail, and if I lose I will have to avenge the defeat out of embarrassment and I will end up in jail anyway.

Either way, I'm too old and too cunning for that. When I had my baby son in my arms I grew into a man instead of being the big kid I have always been. Now I have serious responsibilities and it's frightening. I have given up the smokes, cut back on the grog, got a passport, a driver's licence and an American Express card. Once I had a licence to kill, now I've got a licence to drive. I am a respected member of the community but when I stand in a bar I am a freak and for me it could be a death trap waiting to go off. This being a good citizen bullshit isn't real easy.

THREE DAYS LATER

HAVE seen so much pain and suffering in my life. I have had people die in my arms and die at my hand. I thought I could not sink lower but I was wrong. I have now been lowered into the abyss of Hell.

I have been banned from the only pub in town. The Richmond Arms. Twenty-three years in jail getting pissed on potato peelings and now I have been blocked from sitting on a bar stool shooting the breeze, as compared to shooting a dago.

As usual, dear reader, it all started as a misunderstanding that got out of control. I popped into town for about thirty pots and some bloke thought the fat bloke in the T-shirt with tatts on his arm was an easy target.

There is always a wombat around who wants to be able to tell his mates at the darts club that he laid one on Chopper Read. Usually I can jolly them around and it all ends up with a couple of pictures for their scrap-book and a pat on the back but this time I was, perhaps, just a little bit crankier than usual.

Any rate this bloke wanted a fight and he got it. I belted him and he fell down. Big deal. He was in his early forties and people said I shouldn't flog an old bloke, but pardon me, so am I.

A while back I gave a few twenty-year-olds a tap and I was told to leave the young blokes alone … you can't win, can you?

I suppose I'm to get pissed, tie myself to a chair and let a pack of spastics flog my guts out, then I would be a great bloke. Just because I was pissed people thought I couldn't fight. Wrong. I can still fight, drunk or sober. I have written a letter of apology to the publicans at the Richmond Arms with $50 to buy the wombat a steak for dinner and a steak for his eye. After all, he didn't call the police so he couldn't be all bad.

The barmaids drove me home that night but when Mary-Ann found out what had happened she physically attacked me and I can tell you, she could punch on better than the idiot at the pub the night before. Mary-Ann barred me from the pub as well. Will I have to get Michael Hodgman QC to fight for me again? He will have to leave the Criminal Bar to battle for me in the Public Bar. Will it ever end?

I MUST seriously consider the fact that I am an alcoholic. I must stand up and say, 'My name is Mark Brandon Read and I am an alcoholic,' the only difference is that I have no desire to give up. Time passes by so nicely with a cold one in one's hand. Maybe it is something to do with the name but, like Oliver Reed, I admit I have a problem but will not allow it to interfere with my duties.

I don't beat up my wife, or drink away the food or rent money, I do not lie down in gutters or lay my hands on other men's wives when drunk. I am a totally socially acceptable drunk. I could be a role model for drunks. I should be studied by drunks so they learn how to behave when drunk.

I no longer mix drink and chainsaws, try not to drink and drive and I don't have a gun licence so I cannot drink and shoot. Those who knew me in Melbourne knew that I always had a gun when pissed so they would now look upon me as a saint. Now I will turn the other cheek and walk away ... to another bar.

Those of you who tut tut should remember that Henry Lawson was a drunk and they put his pickled head on the ten-dollar note. So to you wowsers I say pooh to you all and to the barman I say, make mine a double and be quick about it, too.

CHAPTER 17

THE DEAD ARE MANY

'Before I got out of jail I got a letter saying the grave had already been dug for the man who shot Alphonse.'

HAVING fed the chickens and assorted animals around the farm I pick up the paper to find that Gerardo Mannella failed in the fifty-metre dash against killers in North Fitzroy.

Gerry may have been quick, but you can't outrun a bullet. Gerry's brother Vince got whacked about nine months earlier about two streets away. I can remind you all of the movie *Once Upon A Time In America* with Robert De Niro, let's call this *Once Upon A Time In Australia*.

If I told you that since the start of 1998 one man has been single handedly whacking off everyone, including Mad Charlie, Fat Al and the Mannella boys, you would tell me to get back in the henhouse and get the eggs. If I told you that all Italian organised crime was now run from South Australia and headed by a Mafia Don, known as Pauly, you would probably laugh.

What if I told you the seeds of this war started back with my crew and Big Al's crew in the 1970s? Some of Big Al's people have moved to Pauly's side following Gangitano's death. There are others who are now walking dead men. I have no blue with Pauly, and his right-hand man was once part of my H Division Crew. Mad Charlie was very rich when he died, but no one seems to have worked out what happened to his money. Maybe someone got the money to fund a gang war.

Make no mistake the bodies will keep falling but for reasons I don't understand no one seems to get excited. You can find it between the fashion pages and the sports lift-out. They write more about a new risotto recipe than the blood and guts of an underworld war. God help us and pass me a cafe latte.

About eight weeks before I got out of jail in 1998 I got a letter saying that the grave had already been dug for the man who shot Alphonse. Since then the grave has been filled up with dago bodies and Alphonse's killer is still walking around.

Let's make it clear on the long-range forecast. Before this is finished it will make the old Market Murders look like nude mud wrestling. There is a group of whackers who ran around flogging, belting and shooting people when they were part of Al's team. Each and every one of them has been noted and their dance cards have been marked. They will all get a visit and then will head to the morgue.

Take young Gerry. You kill the older brother, then you have to kill the younger one to make sure there is no chance of revenge. The people moving the pieces on the chess board have been playing the game for more than thirty years and don't act out of impatience. There are people walking around Melbourne now who don't even know their movements have been checked and logged. Their killers are just waiting for the call, then they will go to the spot where they know their target will be, take a couple of headshots and move on. Step by step, that whole crew will be wiped out.

In years to come we will talk of the sabre-toothed tiger, the dodo and Alphonse's crew in the same breath, all extinct.

But they won't say the same about Tasmanian chicken farmers.

I was considering retiring from crime writing but from what I have heard I may have a lot more to write about quite soon. Watch this space. There are more bodies to come.

GOODBYE Jimmy the Greek, a small-time bit player in a much larger production. Dimitrious Belias, thirty-eight years old, got it on the 9/9/99 in the carpark of a St Kilda Road office complex. Good postcode, bad head wound.

Mad Charlie called Jimmy the Greek his money mover. He acted as a front man in card games, using Mad Charlie's money, many years ago. He also bought and sold property for Charlie. He also did work for Alphonse and a few others over the years. He was not a full-time full-on criminal. He would go to the edge without getting his hands dirty.

Jimmy the Greek was a small cog in an organised crime wheel, simply part of the machine. He would not be worth a mention except for the way he died. It is just that the death of Alphonse, then Mad Charlie, has made a lot of mice turn into lions overnight. The reserves are now getting a game in the seniors and some of them won't be up to it when the going gets tough.

In the old days Jimmy the Greek could be controlled with a back-hander. The fact that he was put off indicated he had risen to a level where he was important enough to kill.

Some of the shitkickers have been promoted over the graves of their former bosses.

Jimmy would borrow money to gamble. He was a good gambler but he wasn't as good at keeping his word of honour. When he broke his word he may have received a slap in the mouth a few years ago from men who are now dead. Lions can afford to forgive, mice can't afford such grand gestures.

Bang, bang, see you later, Jimmy.

ONE of the more interesting chaps I have come across in my travels was Johnny Higgs – or, as the police call him in their more formal reports, John William Samuel Higgs. He was the so-called amphetamine king of Melbourne. He was about ten years older than me, a real knockabout old hood and a founding member of the Black Uhlans Motorcycle gang.

In 1987 The Jew and myself, backed by a hand-picked team of similar nutters, were all set to grab Higgsy. He was a perfect target for us: a rich, powerful player in the underworld, but no great shakes on his own. Let me put it another way, toilet paper would have more lasting power under stress than Higgs. He was a fat cat just waiting to be collected. He was involved with Alphonse Gangitano and Gilbert Besanko, in what I don't know, but I doubt if it was charitable interests.

But it was Mad Charlie who pulled our coats on that one. 'Higgsy is all right, Chop. Jesus, ya can't kill everyone,' he told me.

'Yes, we can,' said Dave the Jew. Charlie then went on to say how Higgsy was a better friend than enemy but Dave had the answer for that. 'He won't be coming back so the enemy factor does not apply,' he said. It's hard to argue with logic like that.

Then Charlie came clean. 'Look, I'm in business with him and it's hard to make money with a bloke who's dead.' Charlie was providing chemicals to Higgs's amphetamine network and a war would have been bad news.

It was around that time the Besanko and his crew invited me to a footy game at Footscray. Higgsy was supposed to be there but didn't turn up. I suspect he had been warned off by Mad Charlie.

Higgsy was the power when it came to speed but he owed his position to Mad Charlie. One word and he would been in a cellar having his feet warmed with the blue flame of the oxy gear. Mad Charlie had the power of life and death because his crew was made up of psychopaths pretending to be businessmen, not businessmen pretending to be nutters.

By Mad Charlie just keeping his crew in check blokes like Higgsy were able to go one and on. He was the sort who may carry $30,000 to a card game and to people who would take a contract for $5,000 it was easy money, and very tempting.

Higgsy was one of those few knockabouts who mixed with most of the criminal crews in Melbourne. He was known by the Painters and Dockers, drug dealers, bikies and Alphonse's mob. He also seemed to have an interesting relationship with several police. Later he was able to get the drug squad burgled when he needed some information on a witness. It always pays to have friends, and friends who want to be paid.

Higgsy was powerful, he dealt in amphetamines, dabbled in cocaine and did a good a good line in fake American cash.

Higgsy ran the most powerful crew in Melbourne, not the most feared but the most powerful. They weren't the bang, bang, shoot 'em up type of crims, they were cloak and dagger boys – in it for the money, not the fun.

They lived on secrets, not bloodshed. Higgsy was powerful. He could control the street price of speed like the captains of industry control the rise and fall of share prices.

He was smart enough to make sure all his friends made money as he did and he also made sure that his enemies copped a sling. It was then in everyone's interest that Higgsy be on the street controlling nearly twenty amphetamines labs.

He was also smart enough not to be a smart-arse. He may have been nearly as rich as a media mogul but he always looked as if he needed a quid. He didn't brag and boast and get people off-side. He knew how to keep a secret and his left hand thought he only had one arm because it had never met his right.

It took the coppers eight years of solid investigations to get him and although he went to jail for a few years, he's alive and I would think he made enough money to make sure he will be a rich man when he gets out.

He teamed up with Mad Charlie around 1986, around the time he would have known I was about to get out of jail. I wonder whether he teamed up with Charlie as an added form of protection from me. If it was, it worked. I took a lot of money from Higgsy's people over the years but there was never ever any comeback against us. Higgsy knew he was making enough money not to start a war he couldn't possibly win.

In 1987 Higgsy's chief back-up was Shane Goodfellow and Shane couldn't get over me with a pole vault and a step ladder. In the drug world mice can roar like lions.

To head hunters like me, Higgsy was a joke, an easy target, money for jam, yet he survived and got bigger.

Looking back, I don't think he was a mouse who roared like a lion. Maybe he was a lion all the time, pretending to be a mouse.

I PICKED up the paper in July 1999, having completed my chores, and I read that an old mate turned enemy, then a sort of secret mate again, was released from jail. Peter John Allen walked out of Loddon prison in Castlemaine at 9.30am. Waiting for him was a stretched limousine and chilled champagne. Once upon a time I would have loved to stretch his neck but those days have passed.

It was good to see that Peter looked trim and fit, very Squizzy Taylor, in his posh suit and Robert De Niro sunglasses. Trevor Pettingill was walking beside him, looking ten years older than he should, but weeds always age quicker than oak trees. Peter was a little man with a gun and an ego nearly as big as my own. He had a sense of comedy that kept him alive in the valley of death.

I am about to chainsaw eight ton of firewood at $65 to $85 a ton –

Peter would laugh at that sort of small change. Peter and I came from a different world where you would win and lose fortunes nearly every day. It was fairyland stuff. He would lose it and then make some more. Big deal.

I don't think Peter ever set out to be a heroin boss. He always saw himself as a gunman and a standover man but heroin, and the money you can make from it, just sort of got in the way.

He watched his brother Dennis build a multi-million dollar drug empire and go mad along the way. Peter was calm about it and I would suspect he would have always kept a little more in the piggy bank than others suspected.

I am not suggesting that he will buy a timber run and cut firewood, but after a while the game of cops and robbers can get on your nerves.

I will make a prediction. Peter, mate, if you want to jump back into it again, you will have to kill one man who is very close to you. You always trusted no one as a hard-headed gangster, but now in middle-age you may think you need a friend. You don't, not that type of friend, any rate.

I am not advising you to get a cut lunch and a nine-to-five job but don't allow silly Gangitano's dreams to enter your thinking.

You are one of the most together crooks I know, in or out of jail, and all bad blood aside Peter John Allen is a tough, hard, cool and calm thinking machine. He was always a man on a mission.

Peter, you are the head of a big chain but a chain is only as strong as its weakest link and we both know your weakest link is as weak as piss.

I will give you a year to kill the weak link or he will kill you. Better still, walk away. You are a movie star surrounded by cartoon characters. You are an old lion backed up by mice.

Walk away now or, like Alphonse and Mad Charlie, you will be done by people you trust.

They like the way things are and they won't want some old jailhouse Godfather telling them what to do. I fear the band will have to play again – and Peter, keep an eye on the lead singer.

I HAVE a top secret silent phone number that I have only given to a few people, however I think it must be listed in the Yellow Pages under 'Mentally Ill, Please Ring.'

I was getting on with life when the phone rang and it was Amos Rodney Atkinson. Now Amos only ever had a nodding relationship with sanity and it would appear they no longer speak.

He rang me from Wagga Wagga in New South Wales. I would have been more comfortable if he had rung from Mars and his rocket ship had blown a gasket.

His phone was off and it was like talking down a 44-gallon drum. Amos was pissed and I was pissed off. 'I love you, brother, rah, rah, rah, why do you hate me?' he asked.

'I don't hate you, Jesus, I made you,' I told him. He obviously forgot that in the crime world I was Doctor Frankenstein and he had a bolt through the neck.

'Please,' he said. 'In your books, please stop calling me an Abo, it's offensive.'

Now it has come to this. You can talk about slamming someone's knob in a car door, shooting some wombat in the gut, or removing some sucker's toes with a blow torch and that is considered the height of good humour but mention, in passing, that someone like Amos is a bit on the dusky side and you'll get ten years from the politically correct police.

'Chopper, the homicide squad have been talking to me about holding on to people while you cut off their toes.'

'Amos, you are what you are because Chopper Read tells people what you are,' I reminded him.

'You and Dave wanted to be legends, now welcome to fame.'

'Chopper, you're not going to bag me in the movie are you? Dave's a bit worried as well.'

'Look,' I told him, 'If you thought we were pretty good at standing over people you should see these film people. After I signed their contract they can do anything they want. If they want you, me and Dave in green satin frocks standing in front of the docks singing the *Sound of Music,* that is what's gonna happen.

'Now you either are talking to me with the phone down the toilet bowl or your phone is off. You are being questioned for half the unsolved murders in Melbourne and you are worried about whether they will capture the spirit of Amos in the movie.'

'I love ya, Chopper, I had nothing to do with your stabbing in H

Division all them years ago. I hear you're having a son, mate, call him Amos,' he said.

'No, I'm calling him Charlie, after Mad Charlie,' I said.

'Dave and me didn't do Charlie,' Amos said.

'I never said you did, Amos.'

'I love ya, Chopper, and I always will,' he said.

I couldn't help but think that half the underworld headstones of Australia should be inscripted with the words, 'I love ya and always will.'

And so I say I love you, too, Amos, but a thousand miles have travelled between us and we will never meet again. I get these phone calls from old crims desperate to know how they will be portrayed in the film. Now I am a gentleman farmer and I have no intention of shooting a director or a producer over some artistic creative tension. Let the nutcases buy some popcorn and go and see it for themselves.

I NOTE with comic interest that three members of Alphonse's old heroin army have been done for using a shop in Northcote as a front for selling drugs.

Alphonse was into those coffee shops in the late 1970s. It was an old trick. Get some old shop in Brunswick, Northcote, Coburg or Footscray, get a second-hand coffee machine, a counter and half a dozen old tables and you were in business.

You get six old wogs to sit there every day and all night playing cards. Sling them a few bucks and coffee and grappa and they were the best watchers about.

One of the old dagoes would carry a gun for you. Stick up a picture of the Pope and the Italian soccer side and Robert's your mother's brother.

'Could I have a cafe latte and half a gram of smack to go please.'

Before Crown Casino opened Alphonse used the coffee shops for fronts to gambling joints but that has now dried up.

The old wogs at the front were just old trolley pushers from the markets. The joke was that Alphonse would tell them, 'Listen, the heroin is only a sideline, the real money is in the coffee.' Ha, ha.

IT was in early 1973, a few months before Billy 'The Texan' Longley ordered Kevin Taylor to murder Painters and Dockers secretary Pat Shannon, that there were some serious industrial problems around building sites in Melbourne. Big Norm Gallagher, the head of the Builders Labourers Federation, had slapped some ban on that meant the Painters and Dockers recreation rooms in South Melbourne couldn't be finished.

Putty Nose Nicholls, Doug Sproule and Pat Shannon walked into the John Curtin Hotel in Lygon Street to negotiate a settlement with Norm, as gentlemen do. Putty Nose put a gun in Norm's mouth, a .38 revolver it was, and Shannon suggested the green ban should be banned.

'Listen, comrades,' said Norm, which was a bit rude because one shouldn't speak with one's mouth full, but he went on anyway. A deal was struck and the ban was off. Three weeks after the Painters and Dockers building was completed the ban was back on again. Funny that. Years later Norm was to deny the story. He said it was a .45 automatic.

Me and Keithy Faure asked him to slap a ban on building the Jika Jika maximum-security section at Pentridge and he did it for us. Later we asked him to lift it when the conditions at H Division got even worse.

Big Norm did time in 1985 and when he was in the shower with twenty other blokes in A Division he didn't look like some general who controlled a union army. He used Rapid Shave foam, that poofy stuff that comes out all foamy. I used soap and water, after all it was a jail, not a beauty contest. What did he think? Jana Wendt was gonna pop out of the shithouse for an interview?

In 1977 a person very close to me requested I kill Big Norm. The plan was later called off and I was glad it was.

Some important people get talked about all the time and they will never know that they can live or die on the flip of a coin in some drunken conversation by two men who have never even met the target. Big Norm was marked for death over a remark he made on the evening news. I knew it was insanity but I could not say no to the man who asked me to knock Norm. The gentleman in question came to his senses the next day and called it off. I would have done it if I didn't get the call to cancel.

I wonder how different Victoria would have been if I had not got the call. I am glad I didn't head off too early that morning.

THE time has come to pay a tribute to a toe cutter and head hunter of the old school – ten years younger than me but with the same attitudes. Old Norm Dardovski, the Melbourne-Albanian crime boss first mentioned the name of Anton Lukacevic to me back in 1987. I didn't know him from Adamvic. He was a twenty-two-year-old punk tough guy, screaming for a reputation.

Old Norm said, 'Chopper, Anton loves you, he respects you.' I controlled the world Anton wanted to enter and he had the brains to knock first. All he wanted was my blessing and a few words of advice.

I said, 'Tell Anton, just shoot everyone and take their money, toss the rule book out the window, fear nothing, love no one, remember every hurt and never forget a kindness.' As long as his interests didn't conflict with my own I wished him well.

Professional killers, the real cold nutters within Australia, form a small club. They either know each other or know how to reach each other. We (I mean they) don't have a club room or a secret club house but have invisible ties. Count me out, of course, but I am an honorary life member of the house of death, even though I have hung up my guns.

'Mad Tony' or Lucky Lukacevic climbed the ladder of violence and is a target hitter, meaning he picks his mark. One thousand is the same as ten thousand and ten thousand will get you a million-dollar death. Anton has been very lucky and very smart and I should know. After all, I wrote the book. All he had to do was read it. Mad Tony is one of the top three most feared toe cutters in the business. You don't need to know the names of the other two. I will warn him that he has about ten years left to get his money and get out.

Very few head hunters are allowed to retire. Those who do are either really hard or really shifty. Anton is hard and I was just plain shifty. Ha, ha.

Remember, Anton. The one who wins the game is the one who lasts the longest. You have made them drink their own blood and made them pay you for the privilege.

You have learnt from the book of Chopper, but read on, son. You must develop new skills to survive. You must now learn who your friends are because you will need them. If everyone fears and hates you then even mice can turn into cheese-eating lions.

I don't say I agree with your business, but compared with you Neddy Smith was a lady's hairdresser and not a very good one.

Some of your tricks have had me rolling around the floor with laughter. They all want to go to Heaven but none of them want to die.

But be warned, I found that my smiling face saved my life and you don't have a smile. Jesus Christ was the son of God and he still lost a court case and then his life. You've beaten three murder charges in four years and your luck may be running out. Any one of us can be killed.

I was told ten years ago you would be another me when your tail feathers grew. Well, you've made it and now comes the hard part. You have to live the legend. Getting there is the easy part, staying there is the trick.

Personally I think you will end up getting knocked because like Alphonse and Mad Charlie you will stay too long and not see it coming.

Your old mother would have told you to leave a party while you are still enjoying yourself but you'll want to stay until last orders and it will kill you in the end. I hope I'm wrong but you can't sing or dance so what can you do?

I WRITE about bad men and women and you can read about it and if you find it spooky, pull the blanket up to your faces and thank your lucky stars the boys in blue are out there to protect you.

An interesting point about police. They leave the Police Academy with fire in their eyes and the burning desire to do good and lock up crims.

Then after about six years they get a transfer to the superannuation squad and the rest of their careers are devoted to getting up the ladder and getting more promotions.

They want to score brownie points before floating off into the public service sunset. Crims are not the only ones with retirement plans. Coppers give up their gung-ho attitudes and get their thrill playing the public service roulette game.

The tough nuts like Murphy and Rocket Rod and others have left and are replaced by men armed with cardigans. They think a throwaway is a disposable milk carton and a verbal is the opposite of a noun.

Coppers aren't what they were but, then, neither are the crooks. Police learn quickly that the streets should be patrolled by young constables before they wake up how to take short steps.

I mean, getting stabbed, shot, bashed, verballed, slandered, abused, betrayed while being investigated by your own side while upholding law and order and the good of the community ... this is meant to be a career?

CHAPTER 18

FATHER KNOWS BEST

'When I write the truth I am faced with verbal bullets from my critics and real ones from my enemies.'

27 AUGUST 1999. At about 9am Charles Vincent Read was born at the Royal Hobart Hospital. I didn't know what to say or do. It was a caesarean birth. I've seen some worse sights, but I just can't remember when. I held the little baby in my arms and then for the first time in my life, I truly knew what love meant.

I left the hospital that night and had to tell someone the news so I drove to see my mates Shane Farmer and Mario Diienno, pronounced piano with a D in front of it. They are my mates so it was an obvious place to go although Mario wondered out loud whether a strip club was the right place for a new father to be. It was perfect because what was being flashed about was what got me in this trouble in the first place, ha, ha.

Mary-Ann had run around doing the shopping and other chores before the birth. She comes from tough stock but sometimes I think her family takes this stiff upper lip thing too far. I knew a bloke with a stiff upper lip once. Then I ripped it off. I bet you it stung. Sitting there with Mario, a Royal Commission waiting to happen, I thought, isn't it strange, whenever anything happens in my life, good or bad, I end up with an Italian next to me. Thanks, mate.

A FEW DAYS LATER

Baby Charlie is now home. When parking the car in front of the Royal

Hobart Hospital to pick up wife and child I took out the headlight of a posh BMW.

I jumped out all apologetic to speak to the driver who was there to see his wife and baby. He told me he had read all my books and he didn't seem to take the damage too seriously. We shook hands and in my confused state I have forgotten his name. But thanks, mate, we have a lot in common, new kids and the need for panel beaters.

This driving business can be quite traumatic. I have already been forced to take out the rear side window with a hammer when I locked the keys inside the car. I put the poor Ford Falcon through a barbed-wire fence on my own property when I was tired and emotional as a newt.

I have been told that some of the locals want to go roo and wallaby shooting on Read's Run. A quick phone call to my legal advisers indicated they can't do it without my permission and I am not keen on letting them in. If they jump the fence we will enter the murky world or trespass and litigation. I am polite, but I am still a rattlesnake.

I rang Amos to tell him his phone was off; he sounded like he was off as well. I know the federal authorities are showing a great interest in him – he has been described as a 'Person of Interest'.

I suspect this roo-shooting business is just a way of getting the hillbillies back on to my timber lease. If these wombats want a range war then they will need a missing-persons register just for Richmond, Tasmania.

I may not be the toe cutter I once was but I could out think this lot on my worst days. I am giving little Charlie his bottle and he drinks nearly as well as his old man.

I am sitting in the kitchen, it is 12.30am and the wood heater is burning away merrily. My wife has come in to scold me for sipping on a Mercury Light Alcoholic Cider which is only 2.8 per cent alcohol. For goodness sake, I am more than 2.8 per cent myself so what's the problem. It would actually be diluting my alcohol content by drinking this piss. And apples are a local product so I am helping create jobs in Tassie, so there.

Sure I love the occasional drink but so did Winston Churchill and thousands of others who left their mark.

So I have my shortcomings yet, like you, when we are gone we will be remembered for these comic little ventures.

There was a prison officer in Risdon who always said my marriage wouldn't last and here I am with my son smiling and filling his nappy as though it is the height of good humour.

Everytime that screw shut my cell door he would smile as though to say I am out and you are in. I would just smile back for chess is a long game and a pawn can laugh at a king for as long as he likes but he can never win the game.

He was a pawn and I was a king and time alone can win wars. His wife has left him now and he sits alone in his self-made prison. I should feel sad for him. I don't.

As far as the roo shooters are concerned, perhaps I should bring Dave over for a working holiday. Then it wouldn't be the roos being shot, just the local wombats. As my dad used to say, half the bastards need a bullet in the head and the other half need two.

I WRITE and tell the truth but to avoid the hangman's rope so to speak I will alter or twist little side issues to protect myself, and others from the curiosity of the law. If I talk of a body, I will not necessarily inform the reader of the exact location otherwise pesky coroners and homicide detectives looking to go to the next rung on the police ladder will be popping around for a chat. When I write the truth I am faced with verbal bullets from my critics and real ones from my enemies. Words are like magic stardust to be thrown into the eyes of men to confuse and inform at the same time.

The pen is mightier than the sword but in fairness to the sword great things have been done by men and swords. But without the pen the actions of the sword would not be remembered beyond one generation.

Few men have made their marks with pen and sword and I have stumbled into that exclusive class and now I am a father too.

I always swore that as a feared criminal I would never have a wife and children for I knew they would always be the weak link.

I was right, of course. No strength in swordsmanship, however just, can stand secure against a mad man's thrust. Mad men have missions and they don't have homes.

The birth of my son was the final confirmation that I am finished with crime. A man can throw his own life into the fire but not that of his family. I know the truth as I exploited criminals who had to worry about their families. A criminal family man was like butter doing battle with a hot knife.

I wonder what little Charlie will think when he is old enough to read and sees what his father was before he was born. I just hope he doesn't see me as such a fool and I hope he will see that his very life helped change his father for the better.

I don't regret anything, Every drop of blood, every tear, every day of solitude in jail brought me to this place and to my son. It was all worthwhile.

CHAPTER 19

SUCKED IN BY THE MEDIA

'The heroin trade increased six hundred per cent in Perth after US warships made it a regular port of call.'

THIS comes under the heading of a believe-it-or-not story as most of my yarns do. Some armchair critics like to doubt my tales but I am sure I could persuade them if I tapped politely on their skulls with a claw hammer. Personally, I don't care whether you believe this or not as you are already more than halfway through the book and so it's a bit late to worry now.

Some years ago I was approached by a television network for an interview. Naturally they made it clear that they did not pay criminals for their stories. I made it clear that it would be hundred-dollar bills and a fist full of them in cash, no cheques. So, as long as I was willing to keep their little secret so could they.

The young lady doing the story was desperate to get into the big time. We met and had drinks at her motel and gossiped and chit-chatted, rah rah rah. She kept swinging her room key around and the room number was clear. I agreed to all her nitwit ideas and she had plenty.

This chick was a pure Hollywood dream boat. She thought Australia was to be her stepping stone to the big time, and my story was part of the plan. I asked about the cash and she said she had it and not to tell the camera crew. Come back later, after dinner, around 8.30pm and collect it, she said. 'Where?' I asked. 'In the bar?' You must remember I have lived a somewhat sheltered life in these matters, having spent most of my adult life in prisons.

'No,' she said in a strangely throaty voice. 'Come up to my room.'

It was all very cloak and dagger but I played along. I went home after we did a bit of lightweight filming, walkies and talkies, real lightweight stuff. Later, I returned to the motel and went up to her room.

The chick had a mouth like a gutter and the body and face of a photographic model. I didn't let the tough, dirty talk and swearing put me off. She was acting out a role all in order to impress me with an attitude of 'I've done this a thousand times and you don't impress me', but inside she was shitting herself.

Her boss in Sydney had told me she was to give me a sum of money in cash and that's what I was visiting her to collect. Pussy is fine, but you can't put it in the bank. I rang her room and she said to come up.

I went up and she was in a dressing gown, fresh out of the shower, and a bit pissed. She invited me in and we worked our way through a bottle of champagne and generally chatted. Then she started walking about looking in this bag, then that bag and said to me, 'You won't believe this, Chopper, but I've come all the way from Sydney without a condom, have you got any?'

I shook my head. 'No,' I replied firmly (in more ways than one).

'Well, then, it all comes down to trust, you're not gay, you don't use drugs, you're a clean, healthy guy. I've been checked and I'm clean. What do you reckon, do we need a rubber or don't we?'

Was that a trick question? I don't know too many blokes who would knock back the chance to go bareback with a living wet dream. I reckon she'd seen more naked men than me and I'd been in all-male jails for more than twenty years.

To keep a dirty story clean she went at it like a turbo-charged vacuum cleaner. During all of this one of the camera crew rang her room and she spoke to him on the phone about the following day's interview. She was very business-like on the phone while I was doing the business at the other end.

I went home having forgotten all about the money. But the next day, before the interview started, I said to her in private, as she was putting on her make up, 'Did so and so (meaning her boss in Sydney) give you something for me.'

She said, 'Yeah, but I thought we took care of that last night.'

'You're kidding,' I said. 'Fun is fun but business is business.' At that point the ice set in and she handed me the cash like an escort girl who had been told to pay a client, and in my view she was. She was really angry. I mean ice cold. I looked at her and said, 'Jesus, it's not your money, don't lose your sense of humour. I tell you what, let's split the difference, you take half and I'll take half.'

The ice melted and the sun came out.

'Chopper, it's not the money, I don't care about that, it's just that I thought we were friends.'

'We are,' I said, so with a cuddle and a kiss it was all better. We split the difference.

'Don't tell (her boss),' she said.

'What he don't know won't hurt him. Who would believe it anyway?' I said, laughing.

'You'd be surprised,' she replied. 'You can screw who you like in this business, but if you touch the till you're fucked.'

As we walked toward the camera crew I asked her, 'Does much cash change hands in your line of work?'

'More than you think, mate.' she said, 'And, by the way,' she continued. 'You know how we never paid you? Well, last night never happened either, OK?'

I nodded.

Lights, camera, action.

If *Media Watch* only knew the truth. Now I know what a hot exclusive really is. When they say they are taking a live feed I know they mean it. Ha, ha. And, in case anybody's wondering why I'm revealing this after all this time, it's because the young lady in question has publicly dropped so many broad 'hints' about how she got to interview Chopper Read that I feel she hasn't kept up her end of the bargain. A bloke has his reputation to protect.

AS one grows older one likes to check on the family history. I come from a proud dynasty. One of my great-grandfathers died in the snow after coming home drunk and being locked out of the house by his wife, who had warned him if he came home drunk again she would lock him out.

I've collected quite a lot of war photos of uncles, grand-fathers, my own dad and great-grandfathers on both sides of the family. In checking the family tree I've found the Irish and Scottish clans I sprang from, not to mention the Chinese blood that insinuated itself into my pedigree. I got the madness of the Irish, the fighting spirit of the Scots, the inscrutable nature of the Chinese and the hunting nature of a dingo.

The Masonic Lodge and Freemasonry played a big role in my family for generations. The shield of the grand lodge Scottish constitution hangs in my home and a ceremonial Masonic sword hangs near the fireplace.

French blood runs on my wife's side of the family. Doctor Joseph Ignance Guillotin, a Frenchman and high-ranking Freemason, also invented the guillotine. There is a touch of French blood in both my family and my wife's so, in the name of politeness, I won't say what side of the family is related to that noted gentleman.

Do our forefathers dictate the type of men their sons, grandsons and great-great-grandsons will become? I come from a line of hard men, fighters, drinkers, preachers, cut throats, killers, war heroes and gamblers with a few really good bastards tossed in just to upset the flow.

The women in our family were all saints with the misfortune to marry sinners.

Snobbery in Australia is a futile exercise. The class system is a Pommy leftover. The word fag is an English slang public-school word. The fag master, an older lad, regularly buggered junior lads up the bum for punishment.

These bastards went on to sing 'God Save The Queen' and attempted to instil in us all their own class system. However, there would be more raving mental disorders and sex scandals hanging out of the family trees of the British upper class and Royals than all ours put together.

The Reads look positively normal next to the corgi owners from Buckingham Palace. So, to my son who will one day be taunted by the fact that his dad is or was Chopper Read, all I can say to you is, 'Son, whatever your old dad was it's a whole lot better than being someone who wasn't.'

I'm a man who followed nobody, I went in my own direction and other people followed me – mostly into the shit, but they followed me nonetheless.

At the tender age of forty-four I decided to take up karate, then I was offered lessons in Aikido and Judo so I said, why not? I've done my back in and at eighteen stone I need a gentle mind-lifting exercise.

In the old days the only black belt I needed was one to stuff my revolver in. Aikido, the way of harmony, is a defensive art, complicated but graceful, with tossing techniques that use the attackers' force against them. Aikidoists toss an attacker by manipulating the joints. You need strong wrists for this. I've got a grip like a vice so Aikido will do me.

Judo is the first martial art and the least talked about and includes tossing, choking, immobilising, using joint locks. Then Karate. I'll be doing Shotokan, mostly blocking, striking, free kicking, kneeing, elbow, and offensive movements.

There's a lot of free sparring, defensive and offensive moves and I'm glad to say there's head butting.

My teacher, who I won't name, is a former Australian Army SAS chappy. We won't be mucking about. First, he can fix my bad back as he is also a trained osteopath, then he could break it with a karate chop. I will take up Judo, Aikido and Karate. A bit late in life for all this gung-ho stuff. We will see what we will see but not if they see me first. Ha, ha.

In 1987 I won a trophy in kick boxing. It was the Blind Drunk, Heavyweight division in Footscray. I just punched and head butted the bastard into the mat and he was a black belt third Dan, Tae Kwon Do Karate expert. Flexibility is what I want – and to rid myself of this crippling back injury – so as a form of gentle exercise my teacher tells me the martial arts are the go. So why not?

If it goes well I may challenge Mike Tyson to a fight. He may think doing a bit of jail time makes him tough, but I beg to differ. He may think chewing on a bloke's ears is a little dirty while I would suggest it is the height of good manners. He has a couple of tattoos while I've got about a thousand. He throws punches like a machine gun. I've had a machine gun. I could get Dave the Jew to manage me so that if Don King tried to rob me he'd get the lime funeral.

I reckon we could have the fight held inside a jail with only inmates and guards present and the money would come through selling it to pay television. It would rate its socks off and while I suggest Mike may start favourite, I don't think The Jew would let him get through the car park with the prize money.

When I first came out of prison I was just a tough paranoid so, when needed, I hired myself a bodyguard, a professional security fellow formerly of the Australian Army, Dean Petrie.

Mean Dean I called him. A small giant of a man, slightly shorter than myself but twice as thick. He has since rejoined the Army and I feel it would be remiss of me not to mention his name and thank him for his kindness and his friendship to me.

We spent more time drunk together than sober and he failed to protect me from the one cold enemy that could get me in the end ... the grog. But a more loyal and steadfast and stalwart fellow you would not meet in a day's march and I include these few words and his photo by way of thanks. Good on you, mate.

IT was mentioned to me that I might like to remark on the trouble within the world of certain outlaw motorcycle gangs – sorry, I mean 'clubs'. The whole topic is none of my business. Sid Collins was the former President of the Outlaws M.C. and his shooting cost me dearly.

I did mix briefly with members of other bike clubs on my release from prison for light drinkies and general conversation then decided that it was a web and a world I no longer wished to mix in.

You see you either are or you aren't, you do or you don't, you rock or you roll. I've got friends who are, to put it politely, deeply involved in the Italian criminal world, the Albanian criminal world, and the Chinese Triad 14K, but I no longer mix with them. No offence taken, none meant, I've always been full on. I don't socialise at the edge of anything and that goes for the few friends I have had in the bike world.

I wish them well, no offence meant, none taken, I hope. But I've made my decision. No man can walk on both sides of the street at the same time. I've tried that and, believe me, it doesn't work.

The criminal world and the bikie world are not places for tourists. You are either in or out. I don't intend to make any further remarks in relation to motorcycle clubs because the truth is I'm no longer in touch and I'd only be guessing. Or telling the truth, which would be worse, and very bad manners.

The Collins matter taught me to keep my head out of matters that don't concern me. I can't even ride a motorbike, for Christ's sake. God only knows how I ever got pulled into their shit in the first place. A case of, have gun will travel but no more. If you're interested find out for yourself but don't bother asking me. So to Duck and the boys, A.J. and his team, Josh, Clacker, Doughnut and their crew, Chickenman and his lot, to name a few, *via con dios, amigos*. May God ride with you.

Don't shoot me, I'm just the piano player. That goes for you, too, Larry. Let it go, mate, because I have. And to Ball Bearing, don't go spitting the dummy at me just because me and Mad Charlie got friendly with your girlfriend in 1987.

Jesus, mate, if your girlfriend is working at the Daily Planet Brothel I think it's a bit rich to be bagging blokes for getting up her. Some of you blokes need to get yourselves a sense of humour. Anyway, that's all I'm saying about bikies.

Postscript: Sorry, Melissa, but you must have known I'd publish those photos. Jugs like that just have to be looked at, you know that.

WHO was it who said a man who writes books ends up alone without a friend in the world? Was it Truman Capote or Fred Trueman? I can't remember which. Whoever said it, they were right. People are either shitty because you put them in it or shitty you left them out. So for no particular reason I say the following. Most healthy boys have an inborn appetite for adventure. If it does not come to them they will go out to look for it. It is the urge which from the beginning of history has sent men out to explore the unknown, to climb hostile mountains, to sail dangerous seas, in fact to do anything that involves a risk to life.

Captain W.E. Johns, known to one and all as 'Biggles', is one of the other great figures of *Boys Own* type literature. I like to think that in a funny sort of way I've kept up the tradition of rousing adventure tales for those who don't go for the arty farty, namby pamby stuff that bookshops are full of these days. The Captain was always ready to take a pot shot at the enemy, and it's a philosophy I've followed all my life. Correction, used to follow. Now I just read and write about it.

As a matter of fact, I collect Biggles books and boast several first editions. I have twenty-three books in my collection, with the hope of gaining more.

For a boy, Biggles is what life and adventure is all about. I grew up on Biggles books and it didn't do me any harm – if you consider spending two decades inside no harm. On my worst day one was still left with an inner sense of fair play, a strange sense of honour. Coming from a man like me, with my past, such remarks must sound odd, but I did have within me my own sense of justice. As bad as I was, I still saw myself the lesser of two evils, and my victories would even the score of life or maintain a check and balance regarding the status quo. I can recommend Biggles as bedtime reading for all kiddies.

I note that the famous writer Ernest Hemingway and his father both committed suicide. Is greatness passed on from father to son? I doubt it. Is courage passed on? I don't think so. Is intelligence passed on? Not enough. Is evil passed on? Or goodness? The answer is no again.

There are only four lasting things passed on to children: love, hate, baldness and sadness. I received the latter – my publishers got the other three, plus greed. If you pass love on the child will embrace all the gifts and riches life has to offer. If hate is passed on he will grasp all the venom the snake of life spits out. But if sadness is passed on a strange creature walks the land.

A mental and emotional and psychological freak, devoid of love or hate, a sort of empty human. Place a human like that in a criminal environment and you have what I was, an enigma.

It is only when the sadness passes that humanity takes over. So ends the lesson in self-analysis, with maybe one parting remark from Sir Winston Churchill, who said that a cat looks down on man and that a dog looks up to man, but a pig will look man in the eye and see his equal.

I had to laugh the other day when reading RSL President Bruce Ruxton, a grand old fellow, in my opinion. The question was: is he still stiffly opposed to gays in the military?

'We are dead against it,' replied Bruce. 'There is simply no place for queers in the service and it's not just me, it's time immemorial. Once a person is found out in the military that he bats off-side they go for him. He's taunted until you've just got to send him away. That's exactly what happened in World War II. If a homosexual was found in the Battalion he was gone the next day and never heard of again.'

That may be the case in the army, but a favourite homo-sexual comic saying is 'Hello, Sailor' and you don't have to be Einstein to know why.

After I got out of prison in 1998, I had occasion to do a bit of business with a visiting American warship – or, more to the point, some men off this ship.

I won't name the ship but, not to put too fine a point on it, visiting American warships have always been great traders in heroin, cocaine, small arms, ordinance, meth-amphetamine and other interesting products, most of them illegal. Naturally the Australian and Americans governments will poo poo this as nonsense. The military has changed in some ways and, believe it or not, one warship had a female crew that almost out-numbered the men.

One sailor I was involved with on a matter of no importance to this story was a gun collector and trader in small-arms ordinance, not that I was the least bit interested in that, we were simply swapping American and Tasmanian souvenirs.

The point was, this American sailor and his friends were openly gay, and I mean as camp as a row of tents. They told me that there was little trouble with the female crew as they or most of them were also gay. Then they debated among each other. The homosexual percentage population of the ship must be fifty per cent? No no, more said Rudy. Sixty, maybe seventy per cent said Tex, a black Mexican from Texas who talked like Latoya Jackson.

According to these guys the only one who wasn't gay was the captain and they weren't too sure about him. Put the battleship on wheels and they could tow it down the streets of Sydney during the Mardi Gras.

I had occasion to speak to other sailors from other visiting warships and, believe me, she was six of one and half a dozen of the other. Then the French Navy paid a visit to Hobart. A French warship – well, what a show. The whole thing was like a floating drag-queen show. I think anyone who wasn't a poof on that ship could face a court martial. Bloody hell. Hey, Bruce, they don't pull triggers these days, mate, they press buttons. And in the Navy they press the brown one. When they talk of a hot date in the Navy they mean exactly that. This book started off about crime and criminals, and now we are talking about sailors and Nancy boys. Let's get back to Mad Charlie, Alphonse and so on and so forth.

One of the most vicious things I ever did in a street fight was to rip a bloke's eyeball out and eat it or, to be precise, swallow it down with a glass of beer.

Mad Charlie was a great one for latching on to the human nose with his teeth and, as Charlie was being dragged off, taking half the bloke's nose with him. Shane Goodfellow was famous for ripping out eyes in fights and was rumoured to be the man who blinded a well-known radio personality, later to become a gameshow host, in one eye.

I was at that fight on a beach back in the sharpie days. The radio chap, a big bloke, was working for Radio 3AK, a 3AK Good Guy as they called themselves. I got the blame for that lot but without naming the personality involved it was Shane Goodfellow, not me. I was the one who decked you, but Goodfellow gouged your eye.

Now, on to Alphonse. I can't think of one thing, apart from belting Sheilas, that bloke ever did to earn a reputation. Kicking? He was a great kicker when the other guy was down and, yes, I will say he was a master with a broken pool cue, but Charlie and his nose biting got me.

If you have never seen a bloke with half his nose hanging off, well let's put it this way, it's a strange sight. As for the 3AK Good Guy with one eye – you were paid to spin the bloody platters not be the fucking beach bouncer, you one-eyed goose.

Starting a book is easy. Working your way through it is OK but the ending is always the hard bit. I'm trying to end this one but I keep getting side-tracked. Remember when cocaine kings like Pablo Escobar and the Columbian cartels were all just shit we saw on TV? None of it was real.

Then the Cali and Medellin cartels came along. The same yawn. Coke top grade is $250 a gram in Melbourne and getting cheaper and you know who is bringing it in, not Columbians and not up the bums of South Americans.

American Mexicans, members of the United States Navy, bring in heaps of the stuff. The FBI know it, the DEA know it, and the NCA know it, but you know what an Australian city earns in dollars from one goodwill visit from an American warship? Five thousand sailors all cashed up and all the other little extras involved. It is mega dollars, big revenue and so what if a few sailors bring in a kilo or two or twenty of cocaine? One way or the other it's a fucking boost to the economy.

Get this, the heroin trade increased six hundred per cent in Perth after US warships made it a regular port of call. Now cocaine and small arms have been added to the list and while the DEA, NCA and sniffer dogs go through the containers on the waterfront and the airports, Uncle Sam gets the green light.

Of course, what would I know. Laugh it up, I'm just the fat bloke in the white T-shirt. Let's not allow hard drugs to upset international goodwill, hands across the sea and all that sort of shit. Imagine what would happen if customs and the Federal Police set the sniffer dogs on the US sailors. Do you reckon we would be confident of having the US back us up next time? It was hairy enough in East Timor. Don't piss off big brother by showing that our best friends are drug dealers. As always, everyone is looking at the trees but they can't see the wood. You get what you deserve.

AT the moment I'm reading the *Red Beret* by Hilary St George Saunders with a foreword by Field Marshal the Viscount Montgomery of Alamein KG, GCB. It's the story of the Parachute Regiment at War, 1940-45. This is a somewhat rare issue as it would appear the foreword has been written in Montgomery's own hand and is signed Montgomery of Alamein F.M. Colonel Commandant, The Parachute Regiment.

It is the book I read before I myself tried my hand at such insane nonsense and I'm not ashamed to say never ever again. To fall to my death was my greatest fear so, without a word to anyone, I arranged things and confronted my fear. One of my uncles stood in the blazing sun for over twenty minutes while General Sir Bernard Montgomery spoke to the Fourth Parachute Brigade on their way to Tunisia, or so the legend goes. Anyone from the fourth row back couldn't hear a word he said. When he wasn't stuttering, that is.

I still read military history but not as much as I once did. Some of the military books I've collected are quite rare, to say the least, and the tactics and strategy in them are as true today as they were yesterday.

In the criminal world I saw myself as a warlord, a general. In reality I was a mental case. Now I'm a mental-case general writing about the wars that were and the men that fought in them who are no more. I'm afraid that in closing I must quote the great Ernest Hemingway.

'It is too bad there's no way of exchanging some of the dead for some of the living.'

I've known some very wonderful people who, even though they were going directly to the grave, managed to put up a very fine performance en route.

– Mark Brandon Read

BIOGRAPHY

THE SUPPORTING CAST

DAVE THE JEW

THIS is the most dangerous man in Australia. He has killed more than Golden Staph. As a hitman he works alone and I always admire a man who enjoys his work. When he says he's going to take someone out, he doesn't mean for dinner.

The Jew has been blood loyal to me since we were kids but I have to keep away from him if I am to remain clear of jail.

I have made The Jew the Godfather to my son. It is my sort of Israeli insurance. If anyone tried to get to me through my son it would be a fatal mistake. Remember Entebbe?

The Jew has turned the paid hit into a science. He works out the movements of the target and once stayed under the house of a soon-to-be victim living on baked beans and water as he noted the bloke's comings and goings. The Jew lives a simple life and as long as he knows where to get some baked beans and lime he is happy. When his guts start rumbling it's time to stand clear – and not just because he's about to start breaking wind. It's the signal that he has taken another contract.

CHRISTOPHER DALE FLANNERY

A GOOSE with a gun who ended up stuffed. Unlike The Jew, Chris wanted not only to be a hitman, but he wanted headlines as well, which can be a fatal combination. He ran out of control when he got up to Sydney and ended up being knocked. The coroner came down to Risdon prison when he wanted to know the truth and I informed him that Mr 'Rent-a-Kill' was murdered and his body stuffed into a tree shredder. Had a tattoo on his guts with an arrow pointing down that said 'lunch time'. A pretentious plonker who couldn't work out when it was time to pull his head in, so someone pulled it off.

He wanted to be famous so if Shakespeare was a crime writer Flannery's biography would have been called *Mulch To Do About Nothing.*

DIMITRIOUS BELIAS

DIMITRIOUS was a gambler and a spiv well known in the Melbourne underworld. He knew about money and some criminals used him as a front to buy land and investments. In the old days when he got too big for his boots he would get a smack, like using a rolled up newspaper on a puppy when it gets too cheeky.

He did some time over a $330,000 property scam in 1994. He didn't learn his lesson and in 1999 Belias was put off in the car park of a St Kilda Road office complex. He was dressed in a suit and tie when he was shot. At least it saved the undertaker from dressing him later.

ALPHONSE JOHN GANGITANO

FAT Al was once a friend who turned on me in later years. It was a bad move. Many people have hobbies – stamp collecting, train spotting and the like – and I had one, too. It was hunting down Al. He was good at hitting squareheads with a pool cue but he behaved in a far more polite way when he knew I was out. He moved drugs and was in everything that

could turn a quid. He had to be because as his reputation got bigger and his waistline fatter, so did his legal bills. He shot Greg Workman and then had to hide a couple of witnesses. He was a dead man walking and weeks before I got out of jail I knew that Alphonse was soon to lose the breathing habit. He was shot dead in January 1998 in his Templestowe home by a man very close to him. It has started an underworld power struggle that has them dropping like rodents on Ratsak. I'll just tend to my chickens and watch all the geese and the turkeys get lead poisoning.

MAD CHARLIE HEGYALJI

MAD Charlie was a friend who wanted to be a legend. When he arrived from Europe as a thirteen-year-old he said to his mum, 'Where is the Statue Of Liberty?' All he ever wanted to be was a gangster in New York. He went to the Big Apple and stood outside an old nightclub until he saw mob leader Carlo Gambino. For Charlie it was better than meeting Elvis. When Charlie and I ran together we stood over a few massage-parlour owners. In those days he was known as 'The Don'. I wanted to declare war on the big-time gangsters of the day but Charlie had other ideas. He became the major supplier of amphetamine chemicals in Australia and pulled strings behind the scenes. But it wasn't enough for Charlie who wanted to be recognised as a major gangster.

He got the reputation but only after he was shot dead in the front garden of his South Caulfield home on 23 November, 1998. The goose didn't have a tape in his security camera out the front.

No truth to the rumour that an empty tin of baked beans was found under a tree near the front gate.

VINCE MANNELLA

VINCE loved a good night out and went to a coffee shop and a restaurant around Fitzroy on 9 January 1999. When he came home just before midnight he got whacked in his front yard.

He was one of the team of mice who liked to be around Alphonse and were exposed when Fat Al got ventilated. Vince was good fun at times but he had his own violent streak. He once shot a bloke seven times in the gut when he was banned from some pissy cafe card game. What would he have done if he couldn't get into the Melbourne Cup? He and his crew flogged large amounts of food from some coolstores a few months before he was shot. Now it's not just the cheese that's stiff.

GERARDO MANNELLA

GERARDO was the younger brother of Vince. He used to carry a gun but had tidied his act up and worked in the building trade. He made the mistake of mouthing off that he was going to avenge his brother's murder. He was too dangerous to be allowed to live and the people who got Vince had to get him.

Gerry was visiting another brother, Sal, on 20 October 1999 and when he walked out two blokes were there. Gerry knew they weren't there to detail his car so he took off but only got about fifty metres before he was blatted.

And people reckon there's no gang war going on.

JOE QUADARA

JOE was shot dead when he arrived at work at a Toorak supermarket at 3am on a May morning. Now Joe was a good bloke who wasn't a crook but he knew some of the best around. Someone rang me months earlier and asked me if I knew anyone who could put him off. Naturally, as a humble chicken farmer, I couldn't help. It's against the Telecommunications

Act to discuss such matters. Joe was really sick when he was shot and may well have died from natural causes if he hadn't been knocked. I wonder why three major gangsters, including the bloke who shot Fat Al, turned up at Joe's funeral.

LESLIE HERBERT KANE

LES had been out with his missus when he got home to his Wantirna unit. He went into the bathroom to clean his teeth as he knew plaque was really dangerous. Chuckles Bennett, Vinnie and Laurie Prendergast popped up with some special .22 machine guns with silencers made in Sydney for Jimmy the Pom. Rat-a-tat and the holes in his head didn't come from tooth decay. Dumped on the carpet at the front hallway, he was then put in the boot of his own car and driven off. The car and Les were never seen again. The car was crushed and I was told the body went through a meat mincer in New South Wales. If you ever ended up munching on a burger from Griffith and it had a tattoo, that was Les.

Bon Apetit!

PS Laurie later went on missing list too. Some of these nasty criminals play for keeps.

RAYMOND PATRICK 'CHUCKLES' BENNETT

TOUGH and brave, he was the brains behind the Great Bookie Robbery. He had a big fall-out with the Kane brothers that started a blood war in Melbourne. Ray and two of his crew grabbed Les Kane in his house in Wantirna and that was the end of Les. Chuckles and the other two were charged with murder but beat it easy. On 12 November 1979, two coppers were marching Chuck into the Magistrates' Court when a bloke in a suit stood up and shot him. Chuck was shot in the heart. When the ambulance officers got there they couldn't get a tube into his gob because his jaw was locked tight. He never was much of a talker.

The killer was able to escape after someone pulled open a hole in a tin fence down the back. For the police chasing it was one of those cases when everything that could go wrong did go wrong. Now, whose law was that again?

BRIAN KANE

IT was always said that Brian was the one in the suit that knocked Chuckles to even up for his brother, Les. Whatever, Brian started to hit the piss and you can't watch your back sitting on a bar stool. The Quarry Hotel in Brunswick was where he finally got knocked. His gun was in his girlfriend's bag. Now a Gucci handbag might be a great fashion accessory but it won't stop a bullet. Bad move, Brian.

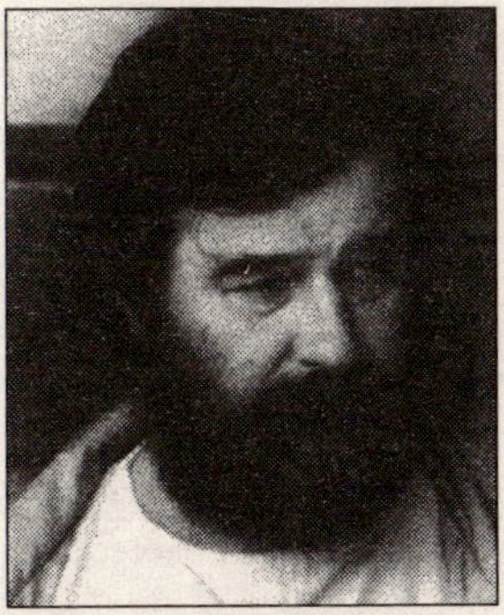

JOHN WILLIAM SAMUEL HIGGS

HIGGS, born in 1946, was in constant trouble with the police as a teenager, with his first conviction at the age of thirteen. He has convictions for theft, stealing cars, assault, manslaughter, assaulting police, resisting arrest and possession of cannabis and firearms offences. He was also charged with illegal possession of a stuffed possum.

It was only to be an apprenticeship. Drugs was the growth industry in his line of work.

He was a founding member of the Black Uhlans Motorcycle Gang, involved in amphetamine distribution for years. Higgs gave the gang its Melbourne club house and is a life member.

He was released from prison in 1978 after serving more than eight years for the manslaughter of a chicken farmer, which was very bad manners.

In 1984 Higgs became a major player in drugs: producing

amphetamines, importing heroin, cocaine and hashish. Around this time he started to pal up with Mad Charlie. Charlie made sure I stayed onside. Better to make money than shed blood, I always say. His gang learnt counter-surveillance, rarely trusted telephones, spoke in codes and only trusted fellow crims they had known for years. It took the cops fifteen years to nail him and by then he'd made more speed than Michael Schumacher and Jack Brabham put together. After eight separate task-force operations, he was still the biggest amphetamine producer in Australia and possibly the world.

There's no doubt that he stayed in front of the posse with the help of inside information. On 20 August 1993, he delayed an amphetamine cook for more than two weeks after he was warned police were about to launch a blitz on the five biggest speed gangs in Victoria. He later got the drug squad burgled and that wasn't done by fairies from the bottom of the garden, unless they wore bad suits and answered to the name Senior Detective.

Higgsy was the sort who wanted things to run smoothly and didn't use violence just for enjoyment but he could get cross when it suited. He took out an $80,000 contract on Daniel Hacking who owed him a $100,000. Hacking later fell from a boat in in Queensland and drowned.

Police made Higgs their number-one drug target and set up Operation Phalanx. It resulted in the arrest of 135 suspects.

Higgs pleaded guilty to one charge of conspiracy to traffic methamphetamine between 1 January 1993 and 30 June 1996. Judge David Jones sentenced him to six years with a minimum of four years, and described him as the principal, key figure, driving force and mastermind of the conspiracy.

Described by his barrister, Roy Punshon, as a semi-literate 'wheeler and dealer', Higgs discovered while previously in custody there were opportunities to be had in supplying the private prison system with various items.

A company of Higgs's had a prison's contract to supply runners, tracksuits and soap powder. Higgsy was able to use his own gear while he was inside. Obviously a business genius.

SHANE GOODFELLOW

HE was once one of the toughest men in Australia. Known as 'Hollywood' he was the heavy in the background for Higgsy. But he got on the gear himself and the needle did what other gangsters couldn't. The curtain came down on Hollywood in 1992 from a drug overdose.

MARY-ANN READ

HERE is a real case of beauty and the beast. She is the light of my life. Without her I would be back in jail. She married me when I was in jail and she stuck with me through thin (when I got out of jail and was on a veggie diet) and thick (when I got on the piss and porked up).

She boxed my ears (ha) when I got banned from the Richmond Arms and entered the twilight zone of the demented when she was pregnant but we get on well together and now have a son, Charlie Vincent.

Chopper: husband, father, straightman. Who could believe it?

KEITH FAURE

AN old enemy. We fought for years over the great sausage war in Pentridge. When he got out he popped down to Tassie for a visit. Once I would have wrung his neck, but now I wish him no ill will. I understand he is now going straight. It looks like some of the old leopards are finally losing their spots. Good luck, Keith, hope you don't run into any 'snags' in future.

ERIC BANA

THE man who got to play me in the movie. I used to watch him on television and thought he had the necessary degree of insanity to play me. He comes from Melbourne and the northern suburbs at that, so is no Nancy boy trying to be a tough guy. He came to Tassie to visit and we got on the piss together. One disappointment was that he didn't get those ears off for the role. Whatever happened to method acting?

PETER JOHN ALLEN

THE best crim I ever met without a proper surname. A jailhouse lawyer and cool customer. We fell out in jail but I still respected him. Part of the Pettingill clan but the only one with balls, brains and a handshake agreement with sanity. He ran a big drug syndicate from inside jail using five TAB accounts. After I left the system he ran the joint. He made nearly 18,000 phone calls from jail when he still ran his drug syndicate. He was released in July 1999 and I reckon it's time he pulled up.

DENNIS BRUCE ALLEN

HEROIN dealer, killer and dog. I should have killed him in prison in the 1970s and saved a lot of people a lot of trouble. He didn't seem a bad kid then but he must have been. As he got more power he turned into an evil bastard. He used to masturbate while killing people. You shouldn't do that because you can go blind. Died in 1987. No loss.

AMOS ATKINSON

AMOS is one of hose blokes that I'll never forget but I must leave behind. He was one of the overcoat gang who backed me in Pentridge and he held thirty people hostage in the Melbourne Italian Waiters'

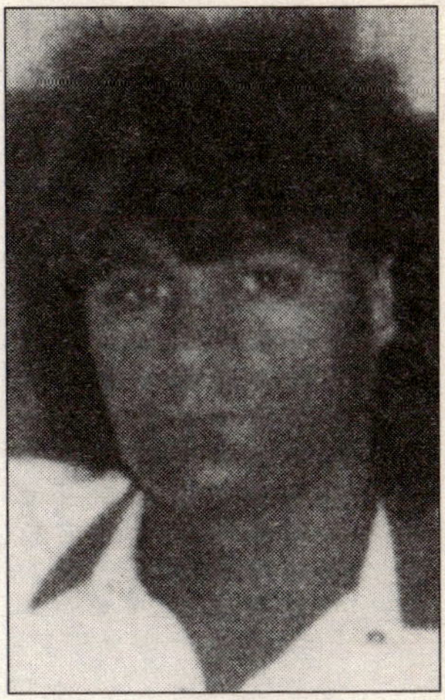

Club trying to get me released from jail. It was a dumb plan. I hope he had the veal parmigiana there, it was really quite yummy.

Amos cut his ears off while in jail with me. Now he lives in Wagga and seems to live in the past. I know he wants to keep in touch with me but I suspect that Amos would be bad news for me because I believe police are interested in him over the supposed disappearance of several hanger-on types in the criminal world.

Good luck, Amos, but you're on your own now.

ANTON LUKACEVIC

A TOE cutter of the old school. Lucky Lukacevic is 'alleged' to have killed three drug dealers in Western Australia and Victoria and beaten each charge when assorted jurors realised it was all a misunderstanding. He has modelled his career on me and why wouldn't you? A hammerhead shark in a school of guppies, he is a real tough guy. He says I am his hero. Well, he should listen to the master and know when to pull up. Toe cutters retire or end up dead. I know which is the best option.

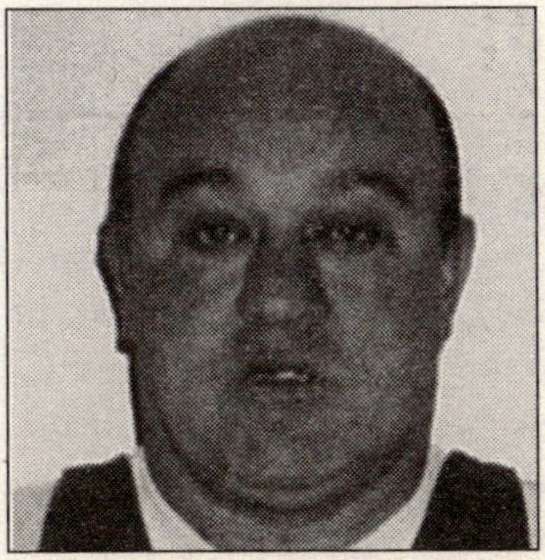

FRANKIE WAGHORN

AN OLD mate who had the biggest right-hand punch in the underworld. He's now in jail for killing a wombat called Johnny Turner. I believe Frankie when he said he wasn't involved. The blood on the carpet may have come from a sleep walking haemophiliac. Ha, ha.

MICHAEL JOHN MARLOW

ANOTHER old friend that I have had to flush out of my life. He has been convicted of rape and beating a young woman in front of her ten-year-old son. He is not due out of jail until 2012. Mick, if you're ever passing my place, just keep driving. I don't like your style and I wouldn't let you near my hen house.

DANNY BOY MENDOZA

DANNY was a Romanian private eye. He mustn't have been all that flash because he didn't see them coming to get him. He was bashed and then shot about five times in the head. A touch of overkill, do you think?

His body turned up near Menzies Creek, near Emerald, just outside of Melbourne in June, 1998. I know who did it but I'm not telling. The Romanians have always liked to go on the high wire without a net.

BILLY 'THE TEXAN' LONGLEY

BILLY was a man who I once looked up to. In return I protected him when he was in jail. We have fallen out when I felt he did the wrong thing in Melbourne over a matter of money. I may be an old chicken farmer, but I can still reach out to the mainland. The money was hastily repaid.

TONY McNAMARA

A GOOD, tough, old-style crim, who was one of the Great Bookie Robbers. He was a man who knew where the bodies are buried. He had friends through the underworld and was well liked but some people didn't like the fact that he stayed loyal to me. He died of a drug overdose in Easey Street, Collingwood, in 1990. I don't believe he was a junkie at the time.

Bad luck or hot shot? You work it out. My brain is full.

THE
END